William Hale Beckford

Leading Business Men of Westerly, Stonington, and Vicinity

Embracing Mystic River, Mystic Bridge, Noank and Ashaway

William Hale Beckford

Leading Business Men of Westerly, Stonington, and Vicinity
Embracing Mystic River, Mystic Bridge, Noank and Ashaway

ISBN/EAN: 9783337236670

Printed in Europe, USA, Canada, Australia, Japan

Cover: Foto ©Suzi / pixelio.de

More available books at **www.hansebooks.com**

OF

WESTERLY, STONINGTON,

AND VICINITY;

EMBRACING

MYSTIC RIVER, MYSTIC BRIDGE, NOANK AND ASHAWAY.

ILLUSTRATED

BOSTON:

MERCANTILE PUBLISHING COMPANY,

No. 258 PURCHASE STREET.

1889.

PREFACE.

In this historical and statistical review of the commercial and manufacturing interests of this section, it has been our purpose in as thorough a manner as was possible to justly describe those enterprises which have contributed so largely during the last half century to the material advancement of these towns. History plainly shows that many large cities have owed their prosperity and growth chiefly to advantages of situation, great influx of foreign people, and similar causes. Of Westerly and the other towns in this section it is pre-eminently true that the genius and efforts of their people, by the single process of internal development, have brought the present prosperity. This fact, that the history of these towns has practically been made almost entirely by her business men, lends particular significance to the close juxtaposition in which the account of her general and business interests are here placed.

MERCANTILE PUBLISHING CO.

INDEX TO NOTICES.

WESTERLY

AND ITS POINTS OF INTEREST

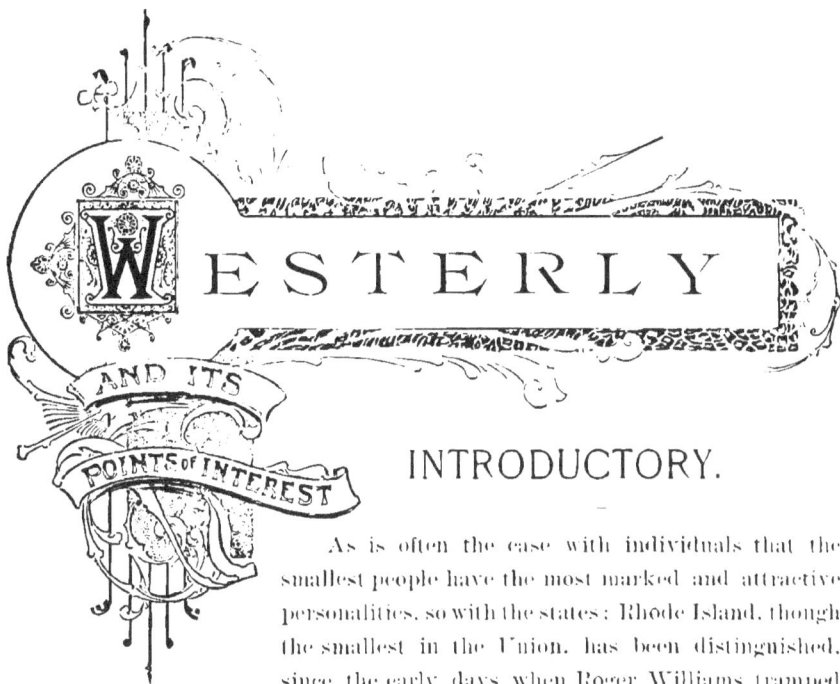

INTRODUCTORY.

As is often the case with individuals that the smallest people have the most marked and attractive personalities, so with the states: Rhode Island, though the smallest in the Union, has been distinguished, since the early days when Roger Williams tramped down here through the wilderness, for certain qualities of sturdy manhood, courage and strength of convictions, resoluteness and tenacity in the councils of the nation and on its fiercest battle-fields. Of all the progressive and characteristic towns that dot its variegated surface and line its winding coast, none have a wider or more deserved celebrity for all that is worthiest in New England life and character than Westerly. Embedded among the granite hills, beautified by the exertions and culture of human industry, and fanned by the cool ocean winds, it forms a most suggestive and attractive theme for the pen of narrator or artist's pencil.

BEFORE AND BEGINNINGS.

The south shore of Rhode Island, at that time called Misquamicut, was inhabited at the close of the 17th century by the Nianties, a rich and peaceful tribe, as were most of the Rhode Island Indians. They were on good terms with their neighbors, the Narragansetts, but were troubled by occasional incursions of the fiery Pequots, who lived to the west of them. To protect themselves from these unquiet aboriginal brethren, they had erected a great fort, just at this point on the Pawcatuck river. They seem to have been quite well advanced into the nomadic or pastoral stage of civilization, and to have possessed such crude elements of the arts as existed among the best class of Indians. They naturally made much of the sea and its finny and shell inhabitants, also of the fine grazing facilities of the country. Their kings were the Ninigrets, famous through New England for their sagacity and kindly hospitable disposition. This tribe never seems to have had any unpleasantness in their relations with the English, though they took but slowly to the latter's christianizing and civilizing influences, and as they did take to them gradually went the way of all the other Indians. The last king, George, was a nominal Christian, and gave quite a large gift of land for the erection of a chapel. After and since his death the government of the tribe was intrusted to a president and council elected by the tribe, the only restriction on whose action was that it must not conflict with that of the state authorities. A scanty remnant of the tribe still exists on a reservation near Charlestown.

The first Europeans to visit Misquamicut were the Dutch who soon after their settlement at New Amsterdam, began to send out trading expeditions along the shores of Long Island Sound. In 1614, Adrian Block in his little bark, the Restless, penetrated as far as Misquamicut. He was accompanied by a Dutch geographer who made a map of this region. If this was perfectly accurate there must have been great changes along the shore since, and no doubt in the last two hundred and eighty years the fierce coast storms have wrought many transformations.

About 1630, as tradition has it, there occurred a very interesting and romantic incident connected with the settlement of Westerly. John Babcock, a young Englishman, came to the house of Thomas Lawton of Newport, then recently colonized. He was employed by the latter and soon took occasion to fall in love with his employer's beautiful daughter Mary, which being reciprocated by her, there ensued some infelicity in the family log cabin. As her father was absolutely implacable the young couple went through the usual method of procedure in a rather unusual way. Having been secretly married, their passion was strong enough to induce them to put out across the rough Narragansett Bay in a small boat; they rounded Point Judith safely, and brought up to anchor in the harbor of Misquamicut. Here they were kindly welcomed by Ninigret, and as nothing further is narrated of them, we may conclude that their days flowed on happily " forever after." Thus felicitously was Westerly founded on a genuine love-nurtured English home.

In 1637 occurred the great expedition against the Pequots of Western Connecticut, who had greatly harassed the settlers of the colonies and in June of that year Capt. John Mason with his brave band of volunteers halted over night with Ninigret at the great fort here, on his way to his great triumph over the Pequots. Ninigret had determined not to send any of his men with the English, but was won over by the skilful arguments of Capt. Mason, and sent

THE DIXON HOUSE, FROM CORNER OF HIGH STREET.

quite a goodly number, who, however, are reported not to have amounted to much in the ensuing battles.

In 1660 the solid foundations of the future town were commenced upon. In that year the whole territory known as Misquamicut was purchased from the Indians by a syndicate of Newport gentlemen, which was composed of Wm. Vaughn, Robert Stanton, John Fairfield, Hugh Mosher and James Longbottom. The bargain seems to have been a perfectly fair one on both sides and it is but fair to say that the original titles to the towns throughout Rhode Island are much better on the average than those of the rest of New England and the country, for they were invariably obtained from the Indians by purchase and that not marked by " vain tricks and dark ways," including the use of beads and fire-water, such as often marred these transactions with the guileless

natives. The little settlement. thus begun by honorable purchase, was colonized in the following year, 1670 and grew steadily though slowly through the
following decade. It received a township charter in 1669, though at that time
it only contained thirty white families. some hundred and fifty people. But
these were the choice of the land and the stock from which New England's
sturdiest heroes came. Westerly received its name, at the same time as its
charter, on account of its extreme western position in the state. We think there
must have been an idea in the minds of its early leaders similar to that of the
great Bishop Berkely when at Newport he wrote:

> " Westward the star of Empire takes it way."

The town of Westerly included at this time the territory now covered by
Charlestown, Hopkinton and Richmond. which were set off later. About 1670.
a Board of Royal Commissioners were appointed by King Charles the Second to
over see the affairs of the American Colonies one of whose functions was the
preparation of charters for the several colonies. Rhode Island included. There
had been some dispute previously about the dividing line between Rhode Island
and Connecticut, but by the charter of Charles II. the boundary line was defi-
nitely settled and Westerly indisputably established in its present state relations. One of the acts of this board of colonial commissioners was the
changing of the name from Westerly to Haversham, which was the name of an
old English town. but this late name never obtained to any great extent and was
soon forgotten. So much greater is usage than decree, royal or otherwise. The
closing years of the seventeenth century were troubled by the horrors of King
Philip's war. Although Westerly did not suffer from any direct attack. for
a long time a constant expectation of such visitation made careful watch.care
and preparation necessary. The militia of the town. which by this time comprised several companies. well trained and equipped joined with those of the
other colonial town in the great struggle for existence with the fierce chief. and
participated in the final victory of the whites at Mount Hope in 1676. The
most important single contest in which the Westerly troops engaged was that
against the great fort of the Narragansetts of Rhode Island under Capt. Church.
During the whole war the Nianties remained quiet and inoffensive. The last
years of the centuries were spent in gradually clearing the forests, enlarging the
dwellings, building churches and school houses, improving the harbor and in
general growth and advancement upon the primitive advantages of the situation.

THE EIGHTEENTH CENTURY

opened quietly and auspiciously. All hostile forces, save those of nature had
been overcome, and although the people had not come into a full realization of
the value of their inheritance, they were of the race accustomed to make the
most of all that was at their hands. A new generation had succeeded to the
original Puritan settlers. but the pioneer blood and spirit still animated those
sturdy souls who had been born in the midst of the undeveloped possibilities of
the settlement. They began to look around them and now the fine fishing and
trading facilities. owing to the coast situation. began to be approximately
estimated. Legislative assistance for the clearing out of the harbor, which had

been much filled up and impeded by the ravages of the ocean storms, was sought and obtained. The size of the fishing and trading craft built here soon began to increase, as these industries developed, and the present town-center about four miles up the Pawcatuck, became the port and marked center of a large and flourishing district stretching many miles back into the country. As the town now steadily advanced in size, different village centers sprang up within it, and the demand for separation soon became urgent, as it was then more than fifty square miles in extent, and all the town government business was transacted in the southern village on the Pawcatuck. After several appeals, the eastern section was divided off in 1738, and incorporated under the name of Charlestown. This latter town being too extensive, was again divided ten years later, and Richmond was incorporated. The northern portion of old Westerly was set off in 1757, under the name of Hopkinton.

In 1740 occurred the greatest religious movement which New England and perhaps the country has ever known. It was called the "great awakening" and was deeply felt and bore large fruitage in Westerly. It took its rise from the preaching tour made by George Whitefield through New England about this time and was marked by great and repeated revivals throughout the colonies. The followers of the "New Light," as it was called, met with much ridicule and opposition from the old established ecclesiastical order, but the movement seems to have been productive of much good. Here in Westerly it resulted in the establishment of five new church organizations. Previous to this time there had only been one regularly organized religious body, that known as the Sabbatarians, or "Seventh Day Baptists." There had also been established here a mission-chapel under the auspices of the New England Society for the Propagation of the Gospel among the Indians, but this was never much attended by the whites. The effect of this great movement in the religious life and future development of Westerly was incalculable and beyond any estimation in numbers or institutions.

As the liberty movement developed and was fanned by the stamp act and other oppressive measures, the citizens of Westerly took an increasingly deepening interest in the great struggle. Their militia which was now organized in three companies, was despatched at the first news of the beginning of hostilities and throughout the war the devotion of the people to the cause was full and unflinching. One of the saddest incidents of the war for Westerly occurred in 1777 in connection with a company which was despatched from this town to aid the expedition of General Sullivan against the British stationed on Long Island. The party from Westerly set out in three large boats and in rounding Point Judith, two of the boats were swamped and fourteen men drowned.

Throughout the Revolution the coast in this vicinity was much subjected to maurauding expeditions by the British, so that a careful coast guard had to be maintained. But the spirit of the people of Westerly was always intensely patriotic and no effort was spared by them which could contribute to the repulse and expulsion of the British. Their volunteer troops participated in most of the great battles of the war and the contributions of the citizens were always generous and prompt. Among other prominent Revolutionary leaders from Westerly were Major General Joshua Bancroft, and also Lieut. Colonel Samuel

Ward, who was especially distinguished for services about Boston during its siege. Col. Ward was a son of Governor Samuel Ward, and like his father was one of Westerly's most distinguished representatives in the state government. Drs. Christopher Avery Babcock and Joshua Babcock, both of Westerly, were among the most eminent surgeons of the Continental army, and performed many notable services. Many of Westerly's most honored citizens fell in the struggle and though their loss was deeply mourned yet the close of the conflict in 1783 was hailed with unfeigned rejoicing. In the organization of the state and national governments which followed, the representatives of Westerly took an active and effective part, and the main body of the citizens sustained

EAST BROAD STREET.

them with thorough loyalty and zeal. The exhaustion of the resources of the people occasioned by the long war necessarily resulted in heavy burdens to be borne in the upbuilding of the affairs of the commonwealth, but none of the resident citizens joined in any such movement as that resulting in the Shay's Rebellion of Massachusetts in 1786. With steadfast courage and their old time perseverance the people turned to the re-establishing of their former industries, in agriculture, fishing, ship-building and coast trade. The closing years of the eighteenth century though not marked by any notable occurrence, were productive of steady growth and advancing prosperity along all the lines and departments of town life.

THE NINETEENTH CENTURY

dawned with every token of uninterrupted progress. The shipping trade was experiencing a great " boom " and all the allied interests of fishing and trading along the coast and with the West Indies at this time were taking great strides forward. But this bright dream of plenty was soon destined to be broken up. The Embargo act in 1807 was a serious impediment to the development of Westerly's dearest enterprises and this was followed by other restrictive measures crippling the town more and more till by 1812, the mercantile affairs of the city were almost at a standstill. Although the war was disastrous to their interests, the people did not fail to show their usual patriotism and contribute both of men and means to the maintenance of the war. The presence of the British fleet near the coast again made necessary the constant stationing of coast-guardsmen; but no nearer disagreeable evidence of foreign interference was experienced than the attack on Stonington by the British fleet in 1814. At the close of the war the town again started on the upward road of progress, and despite some set backs and impediments has maintained its advance steadily up to the present time. Fishing and coast-trading have not been entirely abandoned though not drawing as much attention as formerly, while ship-building has fallen far below its ancient place of importance. Agriculture has been maintained at about the same extent as formerly, though its cultivation has become less profitable as the markets have felt more forcibly the power of western competition. The main line of advance has been in that of manufacturing, one new branch being started after another, and the native mechanical inventiveness of the New Englander displaying itself frequently. No more important event industrially, has taken place than the discovery of the great granite resources of the town, which was made in 1845.

The townspeople were deeply interested in the various movements antecedent to the civil war. Several expeditions were fitted out from here for western colonization during the fourth and fifth decades of the century. There was always a strong sentiment against slavery and this found expression in various channels and meetings before the great outbreak in 1861. When the first summons came to Rhode Island for troops, Westerly was about the earliest to respond. The famous military company here, the Westerly Rifles, enlisted almost to a man at the first appeal, and served through the greater part of the war. They formed a company in the First Rhode Island Volunteer Regiment, and after this was disbanded, enlisted again in the Ninth. Their commander in the first instance was Capt. Henry C. Card, afterward Colonel, and many other well-known and gallant officers came from Westerly's crack rifle team. To all the fourteen different regiments organized in Rhode Island, Westerly contributed its full quota without any delay or murmuring whatever. The town was represented in all the most important battles from Bull Run to Appomatox. It contributed in all two hundred and eighty men; of these sixty-two were killed, died from wounds or exposure in the vile Confederate prisons. The memory of the noble men who sacrificed life for the country has been tenderly and appropriately commemorated. Westerly also contributed generously of its resources to the maintenance of the government and the soldiers. Through the various public channels of benevolence, the town disbursed $22,799.33, this not including many private gifts to the U. S. Christian Sanitary Commission and other such noble organizations and efforts. The ladies throughout were most active in the various departments of aid, for which they were distinguished in all sections of the country.

Since the war there has been gradual advance in many industrial enterprises. Despite the panic of 1873 and the various "hard times" that have occurred since, the business interests of the town have on the whole constantly improved. Various new manufacturing enterprises have been established and many of the old ones have been enlarged and improved. The spirit of intrepid perseverance and most careful planning and foresight which had contributed so much to the material prosperity of the past continue to be the marked characteristics of Westerly's commercial leaders. Not only in mercantile lines has progress been made, but much attention and fruitful results have been given to the various other important interests of the town life. The educational system has been strengthened and developed, the religious organizations have increased

CORNER OF HIGH AND BROAD STREETS.

in numbers and resources and the local government departments, of fire, police, sanitation, etc., have been kept up to the times. In 1880, the population had risen to 5,408 and by the compilation of the next census it will be in the neighborhood of six thousand. In the town proper at present there are four national banks, three savings banks, gas works, three progressive newspapers, four hotels, nine churches of the various leading denominations, a public library, a number of large and finely graded public school, and a high school which is maintained at a high average of scholarship. Among the various business enterprises the most prominent of course are the famous Westerly Granite Quarries. This remarkable granite is well known and highly valued through-

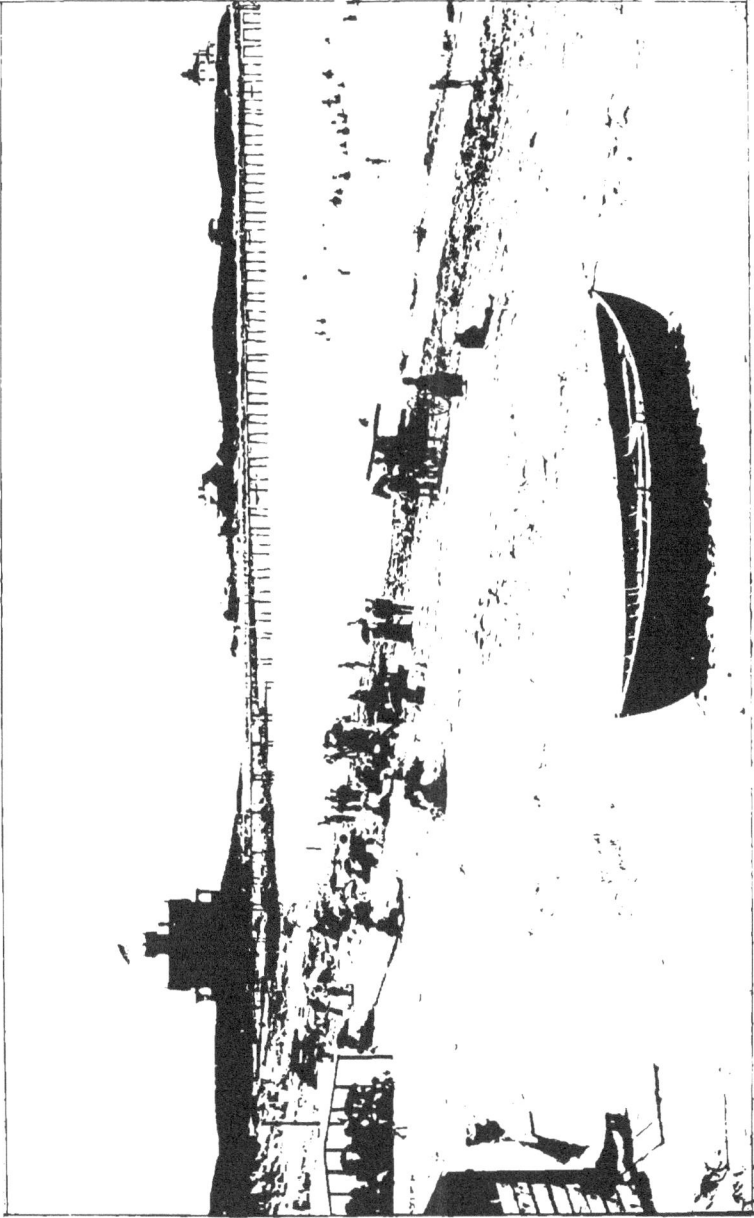

THE BATHING BEACH, WATCH HILL.

out a large part of the country for its superior qualities of delicate shades and
colorings, fineness of grain, susceptibility to brilliant polishing, extreme durability and strength of resistance. It will sustain an average pressure of 19,-
000 lbs. to the square inch, while ordinary granite will not bear much more
than half that amount. Among the most frequent colorings found are those of
red, blue, white and mottled. As some one has observed, there was a vast
source of wealth shut up in these rocky hills of Westerly which its earliest
settlers little supposed to be there, preferring that there had been more level
and fruitful soil. The fact that such a fine lay of granite existed here was first
discovered by Mr. Orlando Smith, in 1845. He succeeded in obtaining a large
part of the land now occupied by the quarries at a very moderate cost and
started the large and important industry which developed the magnificent supply of the stone furnished here by nature. After Mr. Smith's death a corpora-
tion was organized to take control of the industry, which was named in his
honor. There are now in Westerly seven large quarries in operation, employing
from 600 to 1000 laborers upon the immediate works, and 'a large and very
valuable annual output is made. The Westerly granite is sought throughout
the country in all the leading cities, from Boston to New York, to New Orleans
and San Francisco, whenever a work of especial importance requires the very
finest style of stone. Among other prominent industries at the present time
are the manufacture of printing presses, cotton and woollen goods, flannels,
etc. The fishing and coasting trade have revived considerably in recent years.
The town is now the thriving center of a large and prosperous district and is
calculated to grow in size and importance as this whole south-western
portion of the state develops.

The soil varies much, from being in some places composed of a rich gravelly
loam, to others where it is very lean and rocky. It is especially adapted for
grazing and dairy farming is the chief agricultural interest, though garden
farming has developed largely in the last few decades. The town covers about
thirty-six square miles. It is bounded on the west by the Pawcatuck river,
being the last town in Rhode Island on the Connecticut side. It is thirty-six
miles from Providence and about thirty-five from Newport. It is touched on
the south by the Atlantic ocean, and here the coast is very broken, precipitous
and dangerous. There is a tradition that some of Capt. Kidd's treasures are
hidden along the Westerly shore, but it is about as reliable as most of the other
traditions of the same sort. Watch Hill which projects far out into the ocean,
with its long and extremely picturesque shape, is especially dangerous and has
been the scene of innumerable shipwrecks. A lighthouse has been maintained
here since 1806, being one of the oldest on the coast.

Watch Hill, of recent years has become a very popular summer resort.
The picturesque lay of the sea-coast, the comparative retirement and delicious
seclusion, yet easy approach from New York, Boston, Providence, and other
large centers have contributed to give it a widening fame and increasing patronage. It is about five miles from Stonington, and 6 miles from the main town-
center of Westerly, but is easily and pleasantly reached by steamer down the
river or by carriages through some of the most delightful drives imaginable.
When one reaches the point where the long reach of coast, with the sharp point

EAST BEACH FROM LIGHT HOUSE POINT, WATCH HILL.

of Watch Hill standing out abruptly comes into view, the effect is indescribably grand. Over and above the beautiful scenery and fresh, health-giving air from the sea, there are the usual attractions of the ocean side. Fine beaches afford good opportunities for bathing ; the fish are abundant and good facilities are at hand for alluring them landward. Sailing and boating both on the sea and the river are also frequently and thoroughly enjoyed by the sojourners at Watch Hill, the indubitable evidence of whose satisfaction is the regularity with which they come back year after year bringing new comers with them. The multiplication of the cottages which form such ideal homes, has been very marked of recent years. The patronage of the hotels has also been constantly increasing. The hostelries are the Watch Hill House, Ocean House, The Plympton, and its annex, Narragansett and Bay View House, The Larkin and the Atlantic.

The first class advantages of Watch Hill are inevitably calculated to give it an increasing celebrity and prosperity during the coming years and few places can be found so well adapted to satisfy the most exacting visitors and to continually increase in attractiveness as it becomes better known. The interests of the old town are naturally bound up with those of the newer settlement by the sea, and as the charm of the latter's foam-swept shore is woven in with and intensifies the fame of the old and rich quarries, there can be no doubt that the prosperous development of Westerly will continue as firmly rooted as the strong granite hills on which it rests.

LEADING BUSINESS MEN

OF

WESTERLY.

IN the following pages will be found a brief review of the principal Business firms of this section. While the majority are old established houses and leaders in every sense of the word, we have mentioned others who, though recently established, are, through their enterprise and ability, deserving of notice. We commend these firms as a whole to the favorable attention of all into whose hands this volume may fall.

The Smith Granite Co., Artistic Monuments, in their Celebrated Westerly Granite, Westerly, R. I.—It was inevitable that, as the community advanced in culture and refinement, there should have resulted a constantly increasing demand for something besides the stereotyped mortuary emblems with which all had become so familiar, and the manner in which this demand has been catered to, and the taste of the general public elevated by the opportunities given to inspect monumental work combining exceptional artistic and mechanical skill, may be noted with profit by those who affect to believe that all genuine art work must be sought for abroad. When Mr. Orlando Smith began business in 1846, it is not at all probable that he had any adequate idea of the immense development the enterprise was destined to have—a development which is still actively going on, and which has resulted in the building up of a business extending all over the United States. This remarkable growth is due to many causes, chief among which are the enterprise shown in calling attention to the artistic possibilities of the famous Westerly granite from which all work is made, the advance in taste and culture already noted, the high standard of excellence in workmanship, which has been insisted upon from the first, and the appropriateness and originality noticeable in the many designs produced. Since the organization of the Smith Granite Company, in June, 1887, the undertaking has become more widely and favorably known than ever before, for its many departments have been thoroughly systematized, and the most extensive orders can be filled at very short notice. A recent and notable commission was that executed for Ex-Senator James G. Fair, and shipped to Oakland, California, this being a mausoleum, designed and built by the company at an expense of $60,000. Nearly 100 of the monuments at Gettysburg were made by this company, and some idea of the magnitude of its operations may be gained from the facts that employment is given to 375 men, that the yard covers 4 acres, and contains a number of spacious buildings which are heated by steam, allowing the work to go on in winter without interruption, a very extensive plant of steam machinery being utilized. The company has a capital of $100,000, and Mr. Orlando R. Smith acts as president and treasurer, this gentleman being widely known in public affairs, and serving as representative, and as a member of the state board of charities and correction. A prominent and popular specialty with this company is the making of "portrait statues," as they may be called from photographs of the original, the expression and individual characteristics being wonderfully well delineated. Although we have only touched upon the more elaborate work done, we do not wish to convey the idea that only costly commissions are executed, as nothing could be farther from the truth, many modest but beautiful designs being available to choose from at a very reasonable expense. The immense facilities enable all orders to be promptly filled, and no pains is spared to fully maintain the high reputation so long enjoyed by this firm.

E. M. Dodge & Co., Dealers in Ready-Made Clothing, Rubber and Oil Goods, Hats, Caps, Gents' Furnishing Goods, Trunks, Traveling Bags, Umbrellas, etc.; 18th Store of the New England Combination Clothiers; No. 5 Dixon House, Westerly, R. I.—The wonderful growth of the ready-made clothing business, during the past 15 or 20 years, has been often commented upon, and any number of reasons have been assigned for it, but there is no need of seeking far to find explanation of the popularity of a branch of trade which has placed stylish and durable clothing within the means of all. It is doubtless true that dependable clothing was never before so cheap as is now the case, and although the competition, which has brought this about, has, of course, been a good thing for the public, still it has had bad effects as well as good, and has resulted in the placing of a great quantity of clothing on the market, made simply to "sell." There is but one sure way to avoid being taken in by such articles, and that is to patronize only reputable dealers. There are many such in Westerly and vicinity, but not one of them has a higher record for giving full value for money received than the firm of E. M. Dodge & Co., doing business on East Broad st. This concern began operations in 1876, so the public have had ample opportunity to become familiar with the methods employed, and the present magnitude of the business is convincing proof that these methods meet with the approval of purchasers. The premises occupied have an area of 1,500 square feet, and contain a very extensive stock, comprising not only ready-made clothing suited to all ages, but also a full assortment of hats and caps, gentlemen's furnishings, rubber and oil clothing, trunks, bags, etc. Employment is given to 3 efficient assistants, and prompt and polite attention is assured to all, bottom prices being quoted, and every article being guaranteed to prove precisely as represented. Mr. Dodge was born in Westerly, and is extremely well-known throughout this section.

Robert Drysdale, Plumber, Steam and Gas Fitter and Dealer in Supplies 64 Main St. Westerly R. I.—As no subject bears a more important relation to the health of our families than that of sanitary plumbing, we need make no apology for giving it prominence in this book. Every drain pipe, in every house, is liable to be a source of disease, and the only way to make sure that those in your house are not defective, is to have them examined by a competent expert, that is, unless you know, that, they are without flaw, from your own personal knowledge. A gentleman excellently qualified to supervise the construction and repair of plumbing of all kinds, is Mr. Robert Drysdale doing business at No. 64 Main street. He is one of the most thorough and experienced, steam and gas fitters in this town, giving personal attention to every order and thus being able to guarantee that all work entrusted to him will be done thoroughly and economically. Employment is given to only experienced assistants and a large business is done, as Mr. Drysdale's ability is well known and customers of his, feel sure of receiving liberal and equitable treatment.

Barbour's Pharmacy, 18 Broad Street, Westerly, R. I.—"Barbour's Pharmacy" has long held a leading position among the first-class prescription drug stores located in this section of the state, for from the time it came under the control of Messrs. A. L. Barbour & Co., up to the present day, its record has been such as to inspire the utmost confidence in the methods of the management. The firm mentioned above began operations in 1876, and was succeeded in 1888 by the existing concern; Mr. Barbour is a native of Westerly. The premises occupied comprise one floor and a basement, and are of the dimensions of 20 x 50 feet, being located at No. 18 Broad st. A very complete stock of drugs, medicines and chemicals is carried, and the most improved facilities are at hand for the compounding of physicians' prescriptions, to which particular attention is given. Absolute accuracy is ensured by the carefully considered system employed, and orders are filled at short notice, as well as at uniformly moderate rates. A fine assortment of toilet and fancy articles, confectionery, cigars and tobacco is at hand to choose from, and the employment of two efficient assistants assures prompt and polite attention to every caller.

John R. Champlin, Dealer in Boots, Shoes and Rubbers, No. 22 Main Street, Westerly, R. I.—The oldest Shoe Store in town is that conducted by Mr. John R. Champlin, at No. 22 Main Street, for this business was founded in 1844 and has been steadily and successfully carried on ever since. But it is not so much on account of its age that, this enterprise deserves the most prominent and favorable mention that can be given it, as it is the methods which have characterized its past and now distinguish its present management. The proprietor (who is a native of Westerly and has a large circle of friends in this vicinity) does not find it necessary to resort to sensational means to keep up and increase his trade, as he is content with the results attained, by offering strictly dependable goods at a fair margin of profit. It goes without saying that he thoroughly understands his business in every detail, and his customers profit by this knowledge insomuch as they are never offered articles which will not prove as represented. The store is 24x42 feet in dimensions, and the stock carried is very large and complete, a specialty being made of Fine Goods. Apropos of this fact, we would like to call the attention of our readers to the few but valuable hints given by Mr. Champlin concerning Fine Shoes and printed on the back of his business card. He remarks that such shoes are not designed to stand the rough usage given to plough shoes but that their superiority lies in their style, fit and comfort. They are not impervious to water, fire and chemical action and are bound to wear out in time. What is saved in cash by buying heavy, cheap shoes is sacrificed in beauty, fashion and pleasure. Mr. Champlin employs three assistants, and callers are assured prompt and polite attention. Repairing is done in a superior manner at short notice, and moderate prices rule in every department of the business.

The New York Store, John B. Brown, Proprietor, 2 Dixon House, Westerly R. I.— It is now about thirteen years since Mr. John B. Brown opened the "New York Store" in this place, but he had been in business in Westerly in another line eight years previously, and it is safe to assume that the character of the enterprise has been clearly defined and the popular verdict rendered concerning it, long ago. That this verdict is favorable, the present prosperity of the undertaking proves beyond a doubt, and it is not difficult to form an intelligent conception of why the purchasing public endorse Mr. Brown's methods so cordially, as it becomes plainly evident upon investigation that his policy is based upon sound business principles, and consists in a word, of giving full value for money received. This is the oldest established dry goods store in Westerly. He was born in Westerly, and served nearly two years in the army. The stock on hand is made up of dry goods, dress goods, white goods, gloves, hosiery, silks, shawls, handkerchiefs, ribbons, prints, small wares, etc., and is complete in every department, comprising the latest fashionable novelties together with full lines of staple products. Mr. Brown is sole agent for the Butterick Publishing Company's paper patterns and publications, and also represents the celebrated Staten Island Fancy Dyeing and Cleansing establishment, receiving goods at office prices, and returning them with very little delay. His store is located at No. 2 Dixon House, and employment is given to two efficient and polite assistants, every caller being assured immediate and careful attention.

his facilities can be asked for than that afforded by the following list of leading companies represented:

First National, ... Worcester
Equitable, ... Providence
Meriden, ... Meriden
Connecticut, ... Hartford
Merchants', ... Newark, N. J.
Pennsylvania, ... Philadelphia
Niagara, ... New York
Phœnix, ... "
Granite State, ... New Hampshire
Mutual Life, ... New York

James M. Collins, Insurance Agent; 14 Broad street, Westerly, R. I.—A constantly increasing proportion of business men place all their insurance through agents, for experience has proved this to be the most convenient and generally advisable method of procedure, aside from the fact that it is much easier to satisfy one's self as to the character and ability of a local agent, than to carefully investigate the standing of one or a dozen insurance companies located in distant cities. It is a safe rule to follow, that a reputable and responsible agent will not act for corporations in the least degree "shady," for such a man has his personal reputation to maintain and has every facility to get inside information concerning the different companies proffering insurance. Therefore, it is perfectly natural that Mr. James M. Collins should be called upon to write a large proportion of the policies held in this vicinity for he has been identified with his present line of business since 1866, and his record for honorable dealing and careful attention to the interests of customers is unsurpassed. Mr. Collins was born in Stonington, Ct., and is exceptionally well known in Westerly and vicinity. He was clerk of School District No. 1 for 21 years, and is now a trustee of that District, and also an engineer in the fire department. His office is located at No. 14 Broad St., and he is prepared to effect insurance to any desired amount at the very lowest obtainable rates. No better idea of

H. A. Wilcox, Dealer in Fresh and Salt Meats of all kinds, Groceries Provisions, Fruits, Vegetables, etc., West Broad Street, Westerly, R. I.—What is doubtless one of the best known establishments of its kind in Westerly is that now carried on by H. A. Wilcox. The enterprise was originally started by Messrs. Davis & Woodburn, and after several changes in its management, came under the control of Messrs. Green & Wilcox in 1886. Mr. Wilcox assuming full control of the business in 1887. During the many years which this undertaking has been prosecuted, it has gained a high place in the esteem of both large and small buyers, and it is gratifying to be able to state that it never was in a more prosperous condition than is now the case. The premises utilized comprise two floors and a cellar measuring respectively 25x60 and 25x30 feet, and the stock of Fresh and Salt Meats of all kinds, Groceries, Provisions, Fruit, Vegetables etc., on hand is in proportion to the size of the premises, being exceptionally large and complete in every department. Employment is given to four efficient assistants, and pains is taken to give immediate and careful attention to every order. No house in town is better prepared to quote the lowest market rates, and none has a better reputation for supplying goods of uniform quality. Mr. Wilcox is a native of Exeter, R. I., and takes great pride in keeping up the honorable record of the enterprise he controls and is well prepared to meet all competition.

George N. Burdick, Dealer in Lumber, Clapboards, Laths, Shingles, Doors, Sash, Blinds, Nails, Window Glass, Newel Posts, Hardware, and Builders' Supplies, also Brick, Cement, Lime, Hair, and Akron Drain Pipe. Main street, Westerly, R. I.—Lumber and building materials when sold on reasonable terms, means a low priced house, and the more favorable the inducements offered by builders and dealers in lumber and the materials used in the construction of houses, the easier it is for the people to throw off the burden of rent paying and own their homes. Thus the entire community is directly interested in getting such supplies at as low a figure as possible. Quality as well as cheapness has to be taken into consideration of course, but we believe it is generally conceded that at no establishment in Westerly can dependable building stock be purchased to better advantage than at that conducted by Mr. George N. Burdick, at No. 119 Main street, for not only is a very extensive stock constantly carried, but very reasonable rates are quoted on all the commodities handled. This enterprise was inaugurated a number of years ago, and was at one time under the control of Messrs. W. & H. Longworthy, who were succeeded in 1880 by Messrs. Sherman & Burdick, Mr. Burdick becoming sole proprietor in 1886. He is a native of Stonington, Ct., and is extensively known in business circles throughout this section, as he carries on a large and increasing wholesale and retail trade and makes it a point to give equally prompt and careful attention to large and small orders. A two story shop and ample building for storage is utilized. Employment is given to a number of experienced carpenters. Order work done at short notice, and a very heavy stock being carried comprising doors, sash, window glass, shingles, laths, newel posts, clapboards, lumber, nails, hardware and builders' supplies, together with brick, cement, lime, hair and Akron drain pipe.

H. C. Lamphear, Livery and Boarding Stable, Watch Hill, Sunset avenue.—There is no beach resort in this section which can boast of a greater variety of beautiful drives than Watch Hill, and the popularity of this watering place is growing each year. Beautiful scenery is not uncommon in this state and good roads are also to be frequently met with but the two are seldom combined as they are in this vicinity. Occupying a convenient location near the hotels and cottages is the popular stable of Mr. H. C. Lamphear. He has a large number of fine horses and carriages to let, and his stable is very liberally patronized. He has built up his present extensive trade by meeting every demand of the public promptly and at low prices. Horses especially adapted for the use of ladies may always be had here, and luxurious and easy riding carriages are at the disposal of patrons at all times. Horses are kept in fine condition, and those taken to board are assured discriminating care and the kindest of treatment. One only needs to visit the establishment to see that its popularity is well deserved, and its trade is destined to increase from year to year.

H. L. Miner, Dealer in Ready Made Clothing, Hats, Caps, and Gents' Furnishing Goods, Boston Clothing Store; 68 High street, Westerly.—Every man knows how difficult it is to choose a new hat, for by the time the old one is worn out there is always some change in the style, and a very slight alteration in one's head-gear makes a good deal of difference at first. To make a satisfactory choice, it is necessary to visit an establishment where a large and varied stock is carried, and in this connection it is fitting that we should call attention to the Boston Clothing Store, carried on by Mr. H. L. Miner at No. 68 High street, for this gentleman makes a specialty of Ready Made Clothing, Hats, Caps, Gents' Furnishing Goods, etc., and always has a complete assortment of the latest style for his customers to select from. His prices too have much to do with the popularity his store unquestionably enjoys, for they are always down to the lowest notch, and will compare favorably with those quoted at any establishment we know of hereabouts. Mr. Miner is a native of North Stonington, Ct., and has been connected with his present enterprise since 1883. The premises utilized comprise two floors, each 18 x 90 feet in size, and contain a well chosen stock of Gents' Furnishing Goods, in addition to the goods already mentioned. Trunks, Valises, Traveling Bags, Umbrellas, Horse Blankets, Carriage Robes, etc., etc., are also dealt in, and no matter what you buy here, you are sure of receiving prompt and polite attention and of getting the full worth of your money, every time.

Edwin A. Lewis & Co., the High Street Cash and Credit Grocers; Fine Teas, Coffees and Pure Spices; Haxall and St. Louis Flour, direct from the Mill, and Butter and Cheese from the Farm; Hammond Block, Westerly, R. I.—(See cut of building on page 21.) The business carried on by Edwin A. Lewis & Co. was founded many years ago, and passed under the control of Lewis & Brown in 1867, and eight years later the business was assumed by Mr. Edwin A. Lewis, and continued by him until 1881, when he associated himself with Mr. Joseph H. Crandall, under the style of Edwin A. Lewis & Co. They are both natives of Rhode Island and very widely known here. The premises utilized comprise two floors, storeroom and cellar, and are located on High street, (Hammond block.) They contain a very extensive stock of selected staple and fancy groceries, Haxall and St. Louis flour, etc., and an exceptionally desirable assortment of teas, coffees and pure spices, for Messrs. Lewis & Co. make a specialty of these latter goods, and offer grades that for delicacy of flavor and general excellence, are seldom equalled and never surpassed. Butter, cheese, fresh and salt meats, fruits and nuts of all kinds in their seasons are always on hand. Prices are low, and in fact all goods sold at this popular store are offered at the lowest market rates. There are three assistants employed, and all orders are assured immediate and painstaking attention.

HIGH STREET, FROM CORNER OF CANAL STREET.

L. T. Clawson, Merchant Tailor; Woolens and Trimmings; 72 High Street, Westerly, R. I.—Strictly high-grade clothing is sure to be in active demand as long as there are persons of taste and refinement in the community, for such find no difficulty in discriminating between the real and the "make believe" in matters of dress, and insist upon having their garments designed and made by the best-skilled labor obtainable. Now, such labor is expensive, in tailoring as in all other lines of business, and just here is the reason why the so-called "cheap tailors" cannot produce garments that will bear comparison with those made by first-class houses — they cannot afford to employ equally skilled workmen. Mr. L. T. Clawson has built up a high reputation during the past 15 years for furnishing artistic clothing at moderate rates, and a visit to his establishment will prove this reputation to be well deserved, for the garments there produced are certainly unexceptionable as regards cut, fit, workmanship and style, and the prices quoted are as low as is consistent with the employment of the highest skilled labor and the use of the best materials. Mr. Clawson is a native of Plainfield, N. J., and served in the army 3 years, being in charge of the army mails. After being in the merchant tailoring business for 3 years in the West, he came to Westerly, beginning here in 1874. His establishment is located at No. 72 High st., and is well worthy of a visit, if only for the purpose of inspecting the stock of woolens and trimmings there exhibited, for Mr. Clawson makes a speciality of fine woolens, and carries the largest assortment of such goods to be found in the town. The leading foreign and domestic manufacturers are represented, and the variety is so great that all tastes can be suited, the stock comprising the very latest fashionable novelties, as well as those staple products, which are always in demand.

Hinckley & Mitchell, Furniture of all kinds, Undertakers and Embalmers; Rooms, 44 and 46 High street, down stairs, Westerly.—This well known and reliable representative of the furniture business of Westerly was established in 1878, and by reason of energy and enterprise shown in its management, has since attained a prominent position in the trade. This house was first established by J. M. Aldrich, succeeded in 1886 by C. H. Hinckley, and in 1889, the present firm of Hinckley & Mitchell was established. These gentlemen are thoroughly practical business men, and now control an extensive retail trade in furniture. The premises occupied are located at Nos. 44 and 46 High street, and comprise two floors, 20 x 70 and 40x70 feet respectively in size, and a storeroom. These are well stocked with a large variety of furniture of all kinds. Special attention is given to repairing, and all work is guaranteed to be satisfactorily done. These gentlemen are also prepared to discharge all commissions in the line of funeral undertaking and embalming with fidelity and discretion and due dispatch. The individual members of this firm are Mr. D. C. Hinckley, a native of Stonington, Ct., and Mr. H. R. Mitchell, of California, but the latter gentleman has resided in this vicinity all his life. They are assisted by a competent force of assistants, and with unsurpassed facilities and resources, they are in a position to meet any legitimate competition.

C. W. Willard, Stoves, House Furnishing Goods, Farming Tools and Machines, Guns, Ammunition and Fishing Tackle; 22 and 24 High street, Westerly.—A representative establishment of its kind is that conducted by Mr. C. W. Willard, and located at Nos. 22 and 24 High street, and the extent and variety of the stock carried are so exceptional as to entitle the enterprise to the most prominent and favorable mention, especially as the prices quoted are as low as the lowest in every department. Housekeepers, farmers and sportsmen will all find many things to interest them at this popular store, for the assortment on hand comprises Stoves, Hardware and House Furnishing Goods: Farming Tools and Machines, and Guns, Ammunition and Fishing Tackle, besides many

other commodities too numerous to mention. Mr. Willard is also Sole Agent for the celebrated Glenwood Stove Range and Parlor Stove, made by the Weir Stove Co. of Taunton, Mass. No surer way to gain reliable information concerning the latest novelties in any of these lines, can be practiced than to visit this establishment, for the proprietor makes it a point to keep fully up to the times as regards the quality as well as the extent of his stock, and his customers are given every opportunity to become familiar with all genuine improvements. Owing to the rapid increase of trade, they have lately removed to their new and

elegant store. These premises have a total area of about 8,000 square feet, and this large amount of space is fully utilized to accommodate the almost endless variety of goods offered. Employment is given to 5 assistants, and despite the magnitude of the business, orders are filled with a promptness and accuracy which cause the service to compare favorably with that observable in much smaller stores. This business was formerly carried on by Mr. J. H. Porter, who was succeeded by Messrs. Porter & Willard, the present proprietor assuming sole control in 1878. He is a native of Hartford, Ct., and by carefully supervising the many details of the enterprise and sparing no pains to handle only reliable goods, he has greatly developed every department of the business.

———

———

Mrs. Theo. Picard, Dealer in Fancy Goods, Small Wares, etc., 14 Canal Street, Westerly, R. I.—An enterprise that is conducted on strictly honorable and upright principles is that of which Mrs. Theo. Picard is the proprietress. The premises occupied by this lady are located at No. 14 Canal Street, and are of the dimensions of 400 square feet, a full line of every mentionable article in the Fancy Goods and Small Ware line is kept, as is also a well selected variety of Ladies' Underwear and Infants' Wear. A full line of Embroidery Materials, Plushes, Flosses and also stamping done and Embroidery lessons given. Mrs. Picard who is a native of New York Sate became indentified with her present enterprise in 1886, and her style of doing business was so well appreciated by the patrons who were attracted to her tasteful little establishment, that she soon built up an extensive and lasting trade. Only courteous and polite assistants are given employment and all callers may be assured good service, and everything will be found to be exactly as represented. Mrs. Picard is very favorably known throughout Westerly, and all lines of goods offered for sale by her, are quoted at prices as reasonable as can be found in town.

W. E. Stockwell, Dealer in Boots, Shoes and Rubbers. Present location, No. 54 High street, Westerly, R. I.—The demand for footwear that combines style, comfort and durability is steadily increasing, for it is becoming generally known that style and comfort are by no means inconsistent, and that a neatly-fitting boot or shoe is more easy, and with proper usage more durable, than the broad and shapeless productions which were once thought to be indispensable to "solid comfort" so far as the feet were concerned. In the purchase of boots and shoes as in that of clothing, there are some who prefer custom work while others find the ready-made goods perfectly satisfactory, and the magnitude of the trade built up by Mr. W. E. Stockwell, doing business at present at No. 54 High street, is in a great measure due to the enterprise he shows in catering to both classes of patrons, for he carries a large and varied stock of fine boots, shoes and rubbers, and has every facility at hand for the doing of custom work in a superior manner and at moderate rates. Mr. Stockwell is a native of Worcester, Mass., and has carried on his present business since 1879. The premises occupied are 20x58 feet in dimensions, and are very comfortably and attractively fitted-up, while the employment of four efficient assistants assures the prompt filling of all orders. The very latest fashionable novelties are always well represented in the stock, and the prices are uniformly reasonable. Fine repairing is given particular attention, such work being done in a neat and durable manner at short notice.

E. H. Burdick & Co., Pharmacists; 66 High St., Westerly.—Among the many attractive business enterprises of Westerly, none are more deserving of notice than the pharmacy of E. H. Burdick & Co., located at No. 66 High St. The above house is an old establishment, situated in a first class location, having been originally founded by Knowles & Langworthy, later E. H. Knowles. In 1878 the present firm assumed proprietorship, and has since occupied an enviable position in the trade. The premises are spacious and convenient, and the stock shown embraces a full and complete line of drugs and chemicals, together with an assortment of such specialties as are usually to be found in a first class pharmacy. The display of case goods and fancy articles rivals that shown by any of their competitors, and the prescription department is managed with a skill and intelligence which has given the house an enviable reputation in the trade. Confectionery, cigars, tobacco, paints, oils, etc., are largely handled, and warranted to be of first class grades. The firm is made up of Messrs. E. H. & S. C. Burdick, both natives of Westerly. Educated to their profession they have acquired a proficiency that places them in a high position in the trade. Enterprising, reliable, courteous and exact they have secured the confidence of the public to a marked degree, a confidence of which their early training and business career have made them the just recipients.

Windsor House, W. S. Robinson, Proprietor; Livery and Feed Stable Connected; 57 High Street, Westerly, R. I.—Whatever may be the case in other lines of business, it is undeniable that in hotel keeping, liberality always "pays" in the long run. Of course, something besides liberality is required, for careful and intelligent management is indispensable to the attainment of satisfactory results, but this being taken for granted, it still remains a fact that that hotel keeper will be most successful who does not try to get every cent out of his guests that he possibly can. Many instances of this could be given, but we will confine ourselves to that presented by the Windsor House since it came under the control of the present proprietor, Mr. W. S. Robinson, in 1886. This gentleman is not in the hotel business for the fun of the thing, and proposes to make as good a living out of it as circumstances will allow, but while charging fair prices for his accommodations, he takes pains to see that his guests have no good reason to complain of not getting full value for every dollar they spend at his house. It is located at No. 57 High st., and is sufficiently spacious to accommodate 40 guests, the sleeping rooms being pleasant and conveniently arranged, and the beds and other furnishings being kept in first-class condition. An abundance of good, substantial food is provided, and the bill of fare is varied enough to allow all tastes to be suited, the service being prompt and reliable. A good livery and feed stable is connected with the house, and teams may be had at short notice and at reasonable rates. Take it all in all, the Windsor is an excellent house to put up at, and those who go there once will come again when they have occasion to re-visit Westerly.

Oscar Vose, Dealer in Coal, Wood, Hay, Straw, Phosphate and other Fertilizers; Kindling Wood by the Barrel, Oat Straw for filling beds, Hay by Car Load a specialty; Yard on Mechanic street, Westerly.—Newspaper "funny men" have long availed themselves of the opportunity for humorous exaggerations afforded by the trials and tribulations of the man who has to "build the fire" in the morning, and no doubt the subject is comical enough—to an outsider, but to the one whose patience and temper are tried and whose valuable time is lost by wood which won't burn, and a fire which won't kindle, the matter seems serious, and not one to be laughed at. Still a man has only himself to blame for such experience, as it is easy enough to get well seasoned and quick-burning wood if you only know where to look for it, and in this connection we may do some of our readers a genuine service by calling their attention to the enterprise conducted by Mr. O. Vose, on Mechanic street, Westerly. Mr. Vose handles wood and coal of all kinds and is prepared to furnish it in quantities to suit, at very short notice. He carries a large stock and will supply it in any quantity desired. Kindling, straw, and straw for beds is largely dealt in, and a specialty is made of hay by car lots. All orders receive immediate and careful attention, and are assured prompt and accurate delivery.

A. L. CHESTER & CO.

The Model Grand Range. Is equipped with the anti-clinker patent reflex grate: ventilated oven door of an improved style to any now existing; a new double top the strongest and largest in the market; double check damper; the magic kindling ventilating damper; the latest pattern ash sifter, and other improvements so perfectly combined with best material and good workmanship as to make the Model Grand universally acknowledged to be the best Range in the market. A. L. Chester & Co. Wholesale and Retail Dealers in Cotton and Woolen Waste and Paper Stock, Woolen Shoddies of all grades a specialty, Stoves, Ranges, Tinware, Woodenware and Cutlery, 56 High Street, Westerly, R. I.—The enterprise carried on by Messrs. A. L. Chester & Co. really includes two distinct lines of business, for the firm deals very largely in Cotton and Woolen Waste and Paper Stock, and also handles Stoves, Ranges, Tinware, woodenware, Hardware and Cutlery. Both a wholesale and retail trade is carried on, and the premises utilized are very spacious, the warerooms comprising two floors of the dimensions of 25x60 feet, and there being three storehouses containing two floors each, of similar dimensions, additional storage facilities being located on the railroad making something over 10,000 square feet of floor surface, as may be imagined from the accommodations provided, a very heavy stock is carried, and the firm is prepared to fill the most extensive orders at short notice. A

specialty is made of Woolen Shoddies of all grades, and the lowest market rates are quoted on all the commodities dealt in, the mose favorable relations being enjoyed with producers and the great magnitude of the business rendering a small margin of profit remunerative. The firm is constituted of Messrs. Albert L. Chester, Irvine O. Chester and George F. Wells, all of whom are natives of Hopkinton. R. I. Albert L. Chester was born in that town in 1841, and was educated in the public schools and Hopkinton Academy at Ashaway and Berwick Academy in Maine. He taught school a number of terms and in the autumn of 1862, enlisted as a soldier, and served with the 12th. R. I., Regiment until that organization was mustered out. Most of the time since the close of the war, he has been a successful dealer in Cotton and Woolen Waste and Shoddy. In addition to the management of an active business of his own, he has served the town of Westerly as a member of the Town Council several years, as Representative of the General Assembly from May 1879, to May 1882, and as Senator from May 1882, to May, 1885. He is a member of the Republican State Central Committee, a Director in the "Washington National Bank" also in the "Westerly Savings Bank" and the "Westerly Gas and Electric Light Company." He is also both Director and Treasurer in two other corporations. Irvine O. Chester, was born in Hopkinton, Nov. 25, 1859. He was educated in the public schools of that town and the Westerly High School. From 1879, until the formation of this firm he made his home in Exeter. where he was largely engaged in school teaching. He represented that town in the General Assembly from May 1885 to May 1887; held the offices of Coroner and Deputy Town Clerk for several years, and acted as assistant Postmaster at Pine Hill in that town. He was engaged to some extent in insurance and brokerage. In July 1886, he was appointed Assistant Justice of the Second Judicial District, which office he held until his removal to Westerly. George F. Wells the other member of the firm was born in Hopkinton September 7, 1851. He learned a trade as machinist, and worked a number of years for Cottrell & Babcock, manufacturers of printing presses. Later he was engaged in handling Cotton and Woolen Waste, Paper Stock and Mill Supplies. The business office of this firm is at No. 56 High Street, where an attractive display of their wares is made and a sufficient force of assistants employed to insure prompt and careful attention to the wants of every one who may favor them with a call.

Washington National Bank, Broad St. —Westerly is unusually well-supplied with banking facilities, her National and Savings Banks, taken as a whole, comparing favorably with any in the state, but there is not a financial institution in town but what could be more easily spared than the old "Washington" bank, for during the nearly 90 years that this enterprise has been carried on it has become thoroughly identified with every phase of the town's growth, and local merchants and manufacturers have learned to put absolute dependence in the public-spirit, as well as in the financial ability, of the management. The institution was incorporated as a state bank in 1800, and was re-organized under the national banking laws in 1865. It has a capital of $150,000, and from year to year is continually adding to its facilities to carry on a general banking business to the best advantage, while, as may readily be imagined from its long and honorable record, its relations with other banks throughout the Union are of the most favorable character. The Officers and Directors are men who stand high in mercantile and financial circles, and who have proved their faith in Westerly's future by the character and extent of their private enterprise, as well as by their action in connection with the administration of the bank's affairs. The President is Mr. Charles Perry, the Vice President Mr. Nathan F. Dixon, and the Board of Directors is composed of Messrs. Charles Perry, Joseph H. Potter, Thomas Perry, Nelson Brown, Nathan F. Dixon, B. C. Bentley, E. H. Cottrell, Charles Perry, Jr. Mr. Charles Perry, Jr., is Cashier, and Mr. Arthur Perry is Assistant Cashier.

Gavitt's Café and Restaurant. W. B. Gavitt, Caterer. Parties and Weddings Supplied, No. 38 Main Street, Westerly, R. I.— The success of an occasion in which a collation bears a prominent part, is so dependent upon the quality of the refreshments furnished and the character of the service provided, that too much care cannot be exercised in the selection of the caterer. It is hardly necessary to call the attention of the residents of Westerly and vicinity to the facilities at the command of Mr. W. B. Gavitt, for this gentleman is known to carry on one of the best-equipped Cafés and Restaurants in this section of the state, and his ability as a caterer has frequently been demonstrated. "Gavitt's Ice Cream" has long been synonymous with all that is delicious in ice cream making, and the magnitude of his business in this line alone is very great, both wholesale and retail orders being filled, and a specialty being made of furnishing cream for Fairs, Parties, Weddings, etc. The premises occupied are located at No. 38 Main Street, and as they have Telephone connection, orders can easily be sent from any point in town. Suppers will be prepared at very short notice, and "Oysters in every style" is one of the prominent specialties of the establishment during the season. A fine stock of Cigars and Confectionery is always on hand, and low prices are quoted in every department of the business. Mr. Gavitt was born in Westerly, and has had sole control of the establishment since 1888, it having been opened by Mr. I. B. Gavitt about a score of years ago.

Boston Store, J. H. Thorpe, Proprietor. Dry Goods. Small Wares, Carpets. Wall Papers, Window Shades, etc., Broad Street, Westerly. R. I.—It is the easiest thing in the world to give an enterprise any name desired, but to so manage as to make it worthy of its name, especially when that name is sure to bring to mind a high standard of merit, is quite another matter, and J. H. Thorpe, proprietor of the "Boston Store," deserves great credit for his successful efforts to conduct his establishment in a style worthy of New England's metropolis. Mr. Thorpe is a native of Boston, and is evidently thoroughly familiar with the methods pursued by first-class houses in that city, as well as with every detail of his own special line of business. He utilizes premises comprising one floor of the dimensions of 25x110 feet, and a basement measuring 25x60 feet, there being ample room to accommodate a very heavy and varied stock of Dry Goods. Small Wares. Hosiery, Underwear, Cloaks, Shawls, etc., Carpets. Paper Hangings and Window Shades—the Carpet and Wall Paper department being down stairs.—The store is located in Dixon House Block, and is a favorite resort of careful and close buyers, for not only is the stock varied and attractive enough to suit all tastes but the prices are of the "bed rock" character in every instance. Notwithstanding the magnitude of the business, there is no delay in serving customers for fourteen efficient assistants are employed, and immediate and courteous attention is the rule to all. Fresh novelties are constantly being received in every department, and a visit to this popular store is sure to prove both pleasant and profitable.

Milo M. Clarke, Dealer in Beef, Veal. Pork, Mutton and all kinds of Meats and Vegetables in their season, No. 58 Main Street, Westerly, R. I.—Mr. Milo M. Clarke established his present enterprise in 1879, and his methods have resulted in the building up of a large retail business, and the development of the trade is still rapidly going on. Mr. Clarke is a native of Hopkinton, R. I., and is extremely well-known throughout Westerly, where he is Road Commissioner and Assessor. He is evidently thoroughly familiar with the retail Meat and Provision business, for he offers his customers many special advantages, and is remarkably successful in furnishing first-class products that are sure to satisfy the most fastidious. The store is located at No. 44 Main Street, and is of the dimensions of 20x60 feet. It contains a large and well-chosen stock of Meats, Provisions and Vegetables in their seasons. Three competent assistants are constantly employed, this number being increased, in the Summer. The prices quoted are invariably in strict accordance with the lowest market rates. Mr. Clarke gives close personal attention to customers, and his large and efficient force of assistants enable him to fill all orders promptly and accurately.

A. H. Langworthy, Dealer in Flour, Grain, Groceries and Provisions, 32 Main Street, Westerly. R. I.—From the time when Mr. N. H. Langworthy began operations, a score of years ago, up to the present day, the enterprise now carried on by Mr. A. H. Langworthy has been conducted on one invariable principle—the giving of full value for every dollar received. This being the case, it is not to be wondered at that the undertaking should stand high in the favor of the public, and that those familiar with the methods of the management should be out-spoken in commendation of them. The present proprietor is a native of Westerly, and has had control of the business since 1877. He makes no pretensions to selling cheaper than everybody else, and proposes to make a fair profit on the goods he handles, but "fancy prices" are unknown at his establishment, and quality for quality, the rates quoted on the articles dealt in will bear the closest comparison with those named elsewhere. The store is located at No. 32 Main st., and is 20 x 70 feet in dimensions, a spacious storehouse also being utilized. A heavy stock is carried, consisting of flour, grain, groceries and provisions, and employment is given to 2 competent assistants. Mr. Langworthy makes a specialty of catering to family trade, and has had sufficient experience to know just what goods are most popular with this class of custom. Orders are accurately filled at short notice, and a large and increasing business is done.

F. W. Stiles, Photographer, 70 High St., Westerly, R. I.—It is an open secret that the photographic work done at the studio of Mr. F. W. Stiles at No. 70 High St. is not surpassed by any photographer in the state, and this fact, taken in connection with the moderate prices quoted affords ample explanation of the magnitude of the trade built up since the present proprietor succeeded Mr. A. M. Gendron in 1885. The premises are commodious and are very conveniently fitted-up, while the latest improved apparatus and appliances enable all orders to be filled at short notice in a uniformly satisfactory manner, employment being given to three competent assistants and every caller being assured immediate and courteous attention. The high character of the work is of course due in a great measure to Mr. Stiles' personal skill and experience, but a fair share of credit should also be given to the exceptionally complete facilities available, and especially to the effective and original "Lighting Device" employed, the importance of this latter aid being evident to those who have seen it in use, and who appreciate how greatly a portrait is dependent upon the conditions of light and shade. Mr. Stiles invites the public to call and examine his new Glass Mount, whether they wish to purchase or not, and it may be said in passing that a visit to his studio is sure to prove enjoyable, for a beautiful selection of photographic and crayon work is there exhibited. Very low prices are quoted on crayons, and entire satisfaction is guaranteed to every customer, as nothing but strictly first-class work is turned out at this deservedly popular establishment.

Wm. Segar & Co., Dealer in Staple and Fancy Groceries, Provisions and Fruit, 6 Main Street, also Watch Hill Supply Store, Watch Hill, Westerly, R. I.—An establishment deserving to be ranked as representative, not only among the business houses of Westerly but also among the most prominent in this entire section of the state, is that conducted by Messrs. William Segar & Co., at No. 6 Main Street. The business carried on by this firm was founded many years ago by Mr. T. W. Segar, and was continued in 1873 by Messrs. T. W. Segar & Son, who gave place to Mr. T. W. Segar's son in 1879, the existing firm-name having been adopted ten years later. The present concern is made up of Messrs. William and Charles L. Segar, the former being a native of Westerly and a member of the Town Council, while the latter was born in Connecticut. A very heavy business is done, particularly during the summer months, a branch store being maintained at Watch Hill during the season. The main establishment is very spacious, comprising one floor of the dimensions of 40x60 feet, two upper floors used for storage purposes, and a commodious storehouse. The stock of Staple and Fancy Groceries, Provisions and Fruit carried by this firm, is one of the largest and most complete to be found in any retail store in the state, and the goods are selected with especial care, being designed for the accommodation of the best family trade. A specialty is made of Grain, and the most extensive orders can be filled without delay. The prices quoted in the several departments of the business, are the lowest consistent with the handling of first-class goods, while the employment of ten efficient assistants assures prompt and courteous attention to every customer.

S. B. Segar, Dealer in Coal, Wood, Hay, Feed, Grain, Phosphate and other Fertilizers, Opposite Armory Hall, Main Street, Westerly, R. I.—It is very nearly half a century since the business conducted by Mr. S. B. Segar, on Main Street, opposite Armory Hall, was founded, for it was begun in 1841, by Messrs. T. W. Segar & Co. The present proprietor was a member of this firm, and assumed sole control of the enterprise in 1866. He is a native of South Kingston, R. I., and is one of the most extensively known business men in Westerly. A large business is done in Coal, Wood, Hay, Feed, Grain, etc., as well as in Phosphate and other Fertilizers, Live Stock being also dealt in to a considerable extent. The storage facilities available have a capacity accommodating 3,000 tons of Coal, and a very extensive stock of that and of the other commodities mentioned is constantly carried, enabling the heaviest orders to be filled without delay. It is hardly necessary to say that Mr. Segar is prepared to quote the lowest market rates, for his exceptionally long experience in his present line of business has resulted in the building-up of the most favorable relations with producers. Employment is given to five assistants, and a prominent and popular feature of the management is the delivery of orders promptly when promised.

Westerly One Price Clothing Co.
Men's Boys,' and Children's Fine Clothing, Hats and Gents' Furnishings. Potter Building, on the bridge, Westerly, R. I.—The Westerly One Price Clothing Company may be considered among the leading establishments in this vicinity engaged in a similar line of trade. It was founded in 1888, by Mr. Samuel Morris, who is a native of New York City, and is very widely known here. He has gained many new friends since engaging in his present enterprise, for the public are not slow to recognize an evident desire to please, and a determination to deal fairly by all, and these are prominent characteristics of Mr. Morris' management. The premises utilized comprise a store 16 by 75 feet in dimensions, and the stock carried is arranged so as to make the task of selection easy and agreeable. Men's, boys' and children's fine clothing in great variety and all sizes may be found at this popular store, which is located in the Potter building on the bridge, and not only is the cut correct and the goods durable, but the making is exceptionally thorough and satisfactory. Gents' furnishings, hats, etc., are also largely handled, and the prices quoted in every department are so low as to go to explain the high degree of popularity the Westerly One Price Clothing Co., has attained.

A. P. Pendleton, Dealer in Groceries, Provisions, Flour and Grain, 203 Main street, Westerly, R. I.—We need not state our reasons for making prominent mention of the establishment of which Mr. A. P. Pendleton is now the proprietor, located on Main street, for this undertaking has not been carried on during the 51 years of its existence, without becoming familiar to most of our readers at all acquainted with Westerly business enterprises. This house was originally founded in 1838, by Mr. W. C. Pendleton, the present proprietor Mr. A. P. Pendleton assuming full control in 1886. As a first-class grocery store we believe the establishment in question to be unsurpassed, and in some respects even unequalled in the entire vicinity, and we are positive that in no store devoted to retail trade, either in groceries or any other articles is there more careful attention given to the wants of customers and more pains taken to fill every order expeditiously and satisfactorily, and we would refer you to the many customers who have traded here year after year, and it is not surprising that a large business is done, that orders steadily increase from year to year, and that satisfaction is expressed on every side. Such a condition of affairs is but the natural result and although highly gratifying is still richly deserved. Mr. Pendleton carries a heavy stock of groceries, flour and grain, and employs a sufficient number of experienced assistants to enable him to handle his heavy trade without confusion or delay. Special attention is given to the handling of the best grade of articles in the above named lines, and offering the same at most reasonable rates. Mr. Pendleton is a native of Westerly, and holds the office of town auditor.

Miss Sarah P. Wilcox, Parlor Millinery, over O. Stillman's book store. Dixon House Square, Westerly, R. I.—The Millinery establishment conducted by Miss Sarah P. Wilcox, ranks with the leaders in this line of business, not only in Westerly but in the adjoining towns, for this lady does a very extensive retail trade, and the fine stock carried is so large, complete and tastefully selected as to make this a very desirable place at which to trade. The premises are located in Dixon House Square, (over O. Stillman's book store). These parlors have an area of 625 square feet, and are so arranged as to display the costly assortment of millinery goods on hand to excellent advantage. Fastidious purchasers, who find it difficult to obtain articles to suit them at ordinary establishments, should most certainly inspect the magnificent stock here offered, for it is amply sufficient, to supply all tastes. A person doing business on so large a scale as this, must necessarily be in a position to quote the lowest market rates, and customers therefore not only obtain better satisfaction, and more latitude of choice, by buying here, than would otherwise be the case, but save money as well, and there is still another important advantage to be noted, every article is sure to prove just as represented. There are five assistants employed, and all callers can depend upon receiving immediate attention, order work being done at very short notice.

—

O. Stillman, Bookseller and Stationer: Cutlery, Fancy Crockery, Pictures, Frames, Games, Toys, Leather Goods, Druggists' Sundries, Rubber Stamps, etc.; Opp. Post Office, Westerly.—The establishment conducted by Mr. O. Stillman, opposite the Post Office, holds a leading position among Westerly's business undertakings, not only on account of its present standing but also by reason of the many years it has been carried on, operations having been begun by Mr. O. Stillman in 1852. The present proprietor is a native of Alfred, N. Y., and has been in possession since 1882. Premises comprising one floor and a basement, and measuring 30 x 70 feet are utilized, and a very attractive and carefully selected stock is carried, made up of books, stationery, cutlery, fancy crockery, pictures, frames, games and toys, together with leather goods, druggists' sundries, rubber stamps, etc. Employment is given to from 1 to 4 assistants, and callers are always assured immediate and courteous attention, as well as being supplied with uniformly dependable goods at the lowest rates. Mr. Stillman is always on the alert for novelties in this line of business, and his assortment is consequently kept fully "up to the times" in every respect. He also sells passage tickets to and from Europe and the South, by all the first-class routes. Money remittances and drafts are drawn on the principal banks of Europe, and those contemplating a trip across the ocean will find it for their convenience and comfort to call upon Mr. Stillman. Rubber stamps will be made to order at very short notice, and the work is such that satisfaction can be confidently guaranteed to every purchaser.

A. M. Morgan & Co., Architects and Builders, and Dealers in Building Materials; 22 Mechanic St., Westerly R. I.—The vexed question as to whether it is advisable to employ an architect or not in the carrying out of building operations, is not to be decided off-hand, one way or the other, for the matter is entirely dependent upon the circumstances in each individual case. But at all events, it is undeniable that a firm which is prepared to undertake both architecture and building, is in a position to satisfy all classes of customers, and therefore we take pleasure in briefly mentioning the facilities at the command of Messrs. A. M. Morgan & Co., architects, builders and dealers in building material, doing business at No. 22 Mechanic St. The concern was formed in 1887, and is constituted of Messrs. A. M. Mo-gan, T. O. Wilcox and E. A. Morgan, all of whom are natives of Westerly and are widely known here personally. The senior partner served in the army during the Rebellion, and held a major's commission when "mustered out." The firm utilize spacious premises and carry a heavy stock of building materials, enabling them to fill the most extensive orders at short notice, while they are prepared to quote the lowest market rates at all times. Estimates will be cheerfully made, and the concern are in a position to figure very closely on plans and specifications, and to satisfactorily carry out any contract entered into. Plans will be drawn up for buildings of any desired cost, and those who complain that architects are not "practical men," can certainly find no fault with Messrs. A. M. Morgan & Co. on this score, for they combine theory and practice in their business.

J. Beringer, Practical Watchmaker and Jeweller, on the Bridge, West Broad Street, Westerly, R. I.—It is unfortunate that with the great increase of the number of fine watches in general use of late years, there has not been a corresponding increase in the number of those capable of repairing the same, for as matters now are, the better a watch is the more liable its owner is to experience difficulty in having it repaired properly. That this is a correct statement of the case, no one acquainted with the facts will dispute, and therefore we feel that in directing our readers to an establishment where the best work is done in the watch repairing line, we are giving them information which may save them time, money and trouble. Mr. J. Beringer, the proprietor of the place to which we have reference, is a native of England and is a practical Watchmaker and has had a long and varied experience in the repairing of watches and jewelry of all kinds. Mr. Beringer occupies a store on West Broad Street, (with Mr. John Leslie, dealer in Boots and Shoes.) He has been located here since 1886, and those who have a fine watch which is not doing itself justice or which needs attention in any way will find their own interests best served by making Mr. Beringer an early call. He gives personal attention to repairing in all its branches, and his prices are moderate as his work is first-class, and all work is skillfully done at short notice. A well selected stock of rings, spectacles and Watches is always at hand to select from.

Taylor Bros., Dealers in Groceries and Provisions, 25 Beach street, Westerly. R. I. Branch store: Noyes Beach, R. I.—An establishment that has proved very popular in the neighborhood where it is located, is that conducted under the style of Taylor Brothers, 25 Beach street and but a comparatively small amount of investigation is required to ascertain the cause of this popularity. Everybody likes to be sure of getting the worth of their money when they make purchases, everybody likes to know that the groceries and provisions they are consuming are as pure and fresh as the market affords, and everybody likes to receive prompt attention and civil treatment when they have occasion to visit a store and give an order. Now when we say that all these desirable things are to be secured by dealing with Taylor Brothers, we think that no further explanation is needed, of the popularity of the undertaking. Business was begun by Mr. H. G. York, in 1885, he was succeeded by the firm of Taylor Brothers, and the sales have showed a steady increase ever since. The assortment of goods shown includes staple and fancy groceries, meats, flour and grain, drugs, patent medicines, dry goods, etc., etc., in great profusion and of standard excellence. The prices quoted are at all times as low as the market will permit, and employment is given to three efficient assistants, who spare no pains to extend satisfactory service to the public. The business was bought out by Mr. G. B. Taylor in 1888. He is a native of Westerly, and very highly respected among the business men of this town. Mr. Taylor also has a branch store at Noyes Beach, R. I.

I. G. Barber, Manufacturer and Jobber of Fine French and American Confectionery. Main street, Westerly, R. I.—Most of us like candy and ice cream, and most of us prefer home made ice cream to any other kind, for like home made cooking, although not so "fancy" as that made by professionals, still there is something about it that "goes to the right spot" as the saying is, and then we can feel assured that it is pure, and not likely to injure us. Now Mr. I. G. Barber of No. 36 Main street, makes a specialty of making his own ice cream, and he is prepared to furnish it in quantities to suit at very reasonable prices, as you will agree after visiting his popular establishment. He makes it himself, and therefore is in a position to guarantee its purity, etc. If you want fine French or American confectionery, he can supply that too, for he carries a full assortment in stock, obtained from the most reliable sources. Mr. Barber is a native of Westerly, and has carried on his present enterprise since 1885, and has a large circle of friends throughout this vicinity. The store occupied is 20 by 70 feet in size and contains a full stock of fine French and American confectionery, while ice cream, cigars, etc., are largely dealt in, as Mr. Barber is a manufacturer and jobber in the above named line of goods, and does an extensive wholesale and retail business, the leading brands only, being offered at bottom prices. Two competent assistants are constantly employed.

R. A. Sherman, Builder, and Dealer in All Kinds of Lumber and Builders' Materials, 137 Main Street, Westerly, R. I.—During the score of years that the enterprise conducted by Mr. R. A. Sherman has been carried on, it has developed largely in every department, and has come to be considered one of the leading undertakings of the kind in this section. The proprietor is a native of Exeter, R. I., and began operations in connection with his present business in 1869. He is a builder, and dealer in all kinds of lumber and builders' materials, occupying premises located at No. 137 Main st. Various sheds and storehouses are utilized to accommodate the heavy and varied stock on hand, together with a steam planing mill, two stories in height, and 65 x 75 feet in dimensions. This is equipped throughout with the latest improved machinery, enabling the most extensive orders to be filled at very short notice, as employment is given to 30 assistants, and both large and small commissions are carefully and promptly executed. As may easily be imagined from a consideration of the facilities mentioned, Mr. Sherman is in a position to undertake the most extensive building contracts, and to figure very closely on such work, and his record shows that he may be fully depended upon to faithfully carry out every agreement.

S. H. Farnham, Manufacturer of Carbonated Beverages, Nerve Drink a specialty. Canal Street, Westerly, R. I.—It is all very well to declare that water is the "natural drink" of man and that no other beverage is so healthful and refreshing, but the fact remains that water is by no means refreshing during warm weather, unless it is iced, and physicians agree that ice water is so far from being healthful that it is positively dangerous unless very sparingly used. The folly of attempting to satisfy thirst by alcoholic beverages is generally admitted, but pleasant drinks of some kind the public will and must have, and nothing could be better fitted to satisfy this natural demand than honestly made Carbonated Beverages. The cause of temperance has no stronger allies than the manufacturers of these drinks, and the many delicious and wholesome carbonated beverages now on the market are so variously and delicately flavored as to admit of all tastes being suited. Mr. F. H. Farnham is very favorably known in connection with this line of business, for since he began operations in Westerly in 1888, he has attained a high reputation for the uniform excellence of his productions and the low prices quoted on the same. He is a native of Providence, R. I., and is thoroughly familiar with the requirements of the most fastidious consumers, as is proved by the character as well as by the extent of his trade. The premises utilized, are located on Canal Street, and comprise a building measuring 30x75 feet, with an ell 30 feet square. The most improved appliances are used, and great pains is taken in the selection and preparation of the materials employed, the result being that Mr. Farnham's goods are always reliable and are in great request among the trade, his business being exclusively wholesale. A specialty is made of "Nerve Drinks," and all orders are assured immediate and careful attention. Manufactures and puts up in the Patent Ætna Stopped Bottle (the easiest bottle in the market for families to use from) Sarsaparilla, Birch Beer, Nerve Drink, Ginger, Crab Apple Tonic, Orange Phosphate, Lemon and Raspberry soda. All the above are healthful, pleasant and invigorating. If you cannot obtain these goods of your druggist or grocer, orders by mail, telephone, or given to driver, will receive prompt attention. Constantly on hand Siphons of Plain Soda and Vichy for sickness and family use.

Harvey Campbell & Son, Wholesale and Retail Dealers in Coal. Wharf, Main, Foot of Cross Street; Offices, Wm. Segar's Grocery, 161 Main Street, open evenings, Westerly, R. I.—Among the minor evils and inconveniences which at times combine to make the householder's lot far from a happy one may be mentioned that of not receiving articles when they are promised, for it requires but little experience to enable one to realize that the failure of dealers to keep their agreements in this respect may cause considerable trouble and annoyance, to say the least. Especially is this true as regards such bulky goods as coal and wood, and we therefore feel that we are doing our readers a service by directing their attention to an establishment where these commodities are not only supplied at the lowest market rates but where all promises made are adhered to. We have reference to that conducted by Messrs. Harvey Campbell & Son, and are sure that practical trial of the advantages offered by this house will bear us out in all that we have said concerning it. The present firm was formed in 1886, and is constituted of Messrs. Harvey and Fred T. Campbell, the former being a native of Voluntown, Ct., and the latter of Westerly. The senior partner held the position of Assessor for several years, and both members of the firm are well known personally throughout this vicinity. The Wharf has large storage capacity, and is located on Main Street, foot of Cross Street. An Office is maintained at No. 161 Main Street, all orders being assured immediate and careful attention. Coal, Wood and Hay are largely dealt in, and bottom prices are quoted on large or small orders.

———

Campbell, Whitmarsh & Co., Westerly Grist-Mill and Grain Elevator, Grain, Flour, Feed, Wood, Hay and Straw, Custom Grinding, Wood prepared for the stove. C. W. Campbell, J. F. Whitmarsh, C. A. Roby, Grist-Mill Wharf, Westerly, R. I.—The Westerly Grist-mill and Grain Elevator is one of the most generally useful of all our local establishments, and its utility is materially increased by the methods of the concern having it in charge, for they spare no pains to satisfy every customer, both as regards the quality of the service rendered and the lowness of the prices quoted. The enterprise was formerly conducted by Messrs. E. S. Ball & Co., but since 1887 it has been under the control of Messrs. C. W. Campbell, J. F. Whitmarsh and C. A. Roby, doing business under the firm-name of Campbell, Whitmarsh & Co. All these gentlemen are natives of New Hampshire, and give close personal attention to the many details of their enterprise. The premises utilized are located on Grist-mill wharf, and include a two-story mill, measuring 30x75 feet, and run by steam power, a thirty-five horse engine being employed. The firm do Custom Grinding, and also deal extensively, both at wholesale and retail, in Grain, Flour, Feed, Hay, Straw and Wood. Employment is given to five assistants, and all orders are assured prompt and painstaking attention, and accurate delivery at the time promised, while the lowest market rates are quoted in every department.

F. W. Coy, Dealer in Fine Groceries, Fresh Fruit and Vegetables a Specialty. Stores, 60 Main Street, Westerly, R. I., and Bay Street, Watch Hill, R. I.—Mr. F. W. Coy has had long and varied experience in the sale of Fine Groceries, Fruit, Vegetables, etc., and the efficient service he offers to customers affords convincing proof that this experience has been well utilized. He is a native of Westerly, and was formerly a member of the firm of F. W. Coy & Co., but since 1882 has carried on operations alone. Mr. Coy conducts two spacious stores, one at No. 60 Main St., Westerly, and the other on Bay Street, Watch Hill. He does a large business throughout the year, but his Summer trade is exceptionally extensive, as may be imagined from the fact that employment is given to six assistants. The Westerly establishment is 20x 60 feet in dimensions, exclusive of a spacious storehouse, and the Watch Hill store is very commodious, for Mr. Coy caters to the most select trade, and carries so large an assortment that all tastes can be satisfied. His motto —"Quality the test of cheapness"—indicates the nature of the policy which has built his business up to its present magnitude, for he handles no goods that cannot be guaranteed to prove as represented, and grade for grade, is undersold by no dealer in the state. Staple and Fancy Groceries, choice Canned Goods, Relishes, Table Condiments, teas, coffees, etc., are offered in great variety, a specialty being made of Fresh Fruits and Vegetables. Orders are promptly and accurately delivered, and courteous attention is assured to every caller.

———

Albert B. Collins, Pharmaceutist. Dealer in Perfumery, Fancy Toilet Articles, Whitman & Maillard's Confectionery, Arctic Soda and Imported Cigars. Westerly, R. I.—Mr. Albert B. Collins has carried on operations as a Pharmaceutist in Westerly since 1860, and is now located at 48 Main Street. This establishment has long been among the best known in Westerly, for it has been identified with the dispensing of Drugs, Medicine, etc. for the past twenty-nine years, and its record has given it great celebrity. Mr. Collins is an experienced and conscientious Pharmacist, and has given abundant proof in the past of his determination to offer the most reliable service possible to the public. He is a native of Westerly. The premises utilized by him comprise a store 25 x 40 feet in dimensions and a building in the rear for storage, and the stock on hand comprises an exceptionally complete assortment of Drugs, Medicines, and Chemicals, and the compounding of Physician's Prescriptions is given particular and painstaking attention. The facilities at hand for the filling of orders of this kind are of the most improved and efficient type, and customers are spared all unnecessary delay, while the charges are moderate in every case. A fine assortment of Perfumery, Fancy Toilet Articles, Confectionery, Soda and Imported Cigars is always to be found here, and the prices quoted will bear the severest examination and comparison. Two competent and courteous assistants are employed, and all patrons are served in a most satisfactory manner.

M. S. Greene, Insurance and Real Estate Agent, No. 6 High Street, Stillman's Building, Westerly, R. I.—The only question relating to insurance that may be said to still remain an open one, is as to where insurance may be placed to the best advantage, for it has long since been settled that insurance of some kind is a necessity, and we do not propose to bore our readers with the familiar arguments in support of the obtaining of such protection. So large a proportion of the policies written nowadays are issued through agencies, that the question is narrowed down to a choice of these, and certainly, so far as Westerly is concerned, no agency can make a more favorable showing than that carried on by Mr. M. S. Greene, at No. 6 High st., Stillman's Building. It was opened many years ago by Messrs. Collins & Greene, present proprietor assuming sole control in 1879. He represents some of the strongest fire, marine, life and accident companies in the world, and gives prompt and careful attention to all business with which he may be entrusted, being prepared to furnish strictly dependable insurance at the lowest market rates. The following is a list of companies represented:

Liverpool & London & Globe, England.
Norwich Union, "
Imperial, "
Northern, "
Guardian, "
London, "
Phœnix, "
British American, Canada.
Hanover, New York.
Williamsburgh City, "
Westchester, "
Orient, Hartford.
American, Phila.
Insurance Co., State of Penn., "
Providence Washington, Providence.
Traders, Chicago.
Union, California.
Traders & Mechanics Mutual, Lowell.
Pawtucket Mutual, Pawtucket.
Fidelity & Casualty, New York.
Equitable Life Ins. Co., "
Equitable Mortgage Co., "

Mr. Greene also handles bonds and mortgages, and deals in real-estate, having some very desirable property for sale and to let, and is in a position to successfully negotiate loans of any desired amount.

Schofield Bros., Photographers, 30 Main Street, Westerly, R. I. — The great progress made in photography during the past ten years is a matter of common knowledge, and it is hardly necessary to say that work, which would have given entire satisfaction in 1879, would hardly "pass muster" at the present day with the critical public. It is a curious fact that a few photographers seem to be about the only ones who are not conversant with the progress in question, or at all events, if they do know of it, they show no signs of it in their work, but are content to abide by old methods, and consequently by old results. The only thing that enables them to get a living is their practice of quoting very low prices, for there are some persons who will accept anything in the shape of a photograph, provided they get it cheap enough. Such pictures are really not cheap for they are worthless, and a worthless picture is certainly dear at any price. Not that we mean to argue that high prices must be paid to get good photographic work, but there is reason in everything, and the careful buyer will avoid both extremes. In this connection, we may properly call attention to the results attained at the studio of Schofield Bros., No. 30 Main st., for we believe no better work is done in the state than that produced here, and yet the prices are uniformly moderate. This establishment was opened in 1879 by Messrs. Schofield Brothers, and has gained a high and extended reputation. The present proprietor is a native of Westerly, and gives careful personal attention to every order, sparing no pains to maintain the leading position the enterprise attained under its original management. The most improved facilities are at hand for the carrying on of photography in all its branches, and crayon work, etc., is done in the most artistic manner at moderate rates. Callers are assured immediate and polite attention.

Walter Price & Co., Druggists; Dealers and Jobbers in Pills, Plasters, Perfumery, Hair Oil, Pomades, Seidlitz Powders, Horse Powders, Insect Powder, Tooth Powder, Pencils, Arabian Balsam, Atwood's Bitters, etc., etc.; Branch Store at Watch Hill, Westerly, R. I.—In every community of any size there are certain pharmacies which have a specially high reputation in connection with the compounding of physicians' prescriptions, and as this reputation is almost invariably the result of years of faithful service and prompt and accurate filling of orders, it is obvious that those patronizing such establishments have good reason to feel perfect confidence in the skill and care of the management. In this connection, it is appropriate that mention should be made of the pharmacy conducted by Messrs. Walter Price & Co., for this firm have every facility at their command to enable prescriptions to be compounded with perfect accuracy at the shortest possible notice, and as they quote uniformly moderate rates, the superior service afforded is within the means of all. The partners are Messrs. Walter Price, Charles T. Price and T. J. Bannon, the latter gentleman being a native of this state, while both his associates were born in Connecticut. Mr. Walter Price served 3 years in the army. The present firm was formed in 1877, and succeeded Messrs. E. G. Champlin & Co., who had carried on the business for many years. The premises occupied at Westerly are 2 floors comprising a space of 75 x 40 feet in dimensions. The Watch Hill store is 20 x 40, and contains a very extensive and complete stock, comprising one of the fullest assortments of drugs, medicines and chemicals in the state, besides an attractive selection of druggists' sundries, cigars, confectionery, etc. Employment is given to 6 assistants, and callers are waited upon promptly and courteously at all times, while the prices quoted in the several departments of the business will bear the closest comparison with those elsewhere.

men's furnishings, etc. Some of Mr. Babcock's specialties, as for instance the shirt he sells for 45 cents. have a more than local reputation, and it is everywhere conceded that whatever he offers as a bargain, is sure to prove one in fact as well as in name. He is agent for Messrs. G. W. Simmons & Co.'s custom order clothing, and those who prefer to have their garments made from measure can thus, by calling at his store, have the resources of the most completely equipped merchant tailoring establishment in New England placed at their disposal. Fit, goods and workmanship are fully guaranteed and the prices are away down to the bottom. Mr. Babcock employs four efficient assistants, and all callers are sure of receiving prompt, courteous and painstaking attention.

Geo. H. Babcock, Clothier, Hatter and Gents' Furnisher. The home of the 45 cent shirt. Agent for G. W. Simmons & Co., Custom Order Clothing. 16 and 18 Main street, Westerly, R. I.—The day of fancy prices on fashionable clothing has gone by, and although there are still some men who gauge the excellence of a garment by its cost alone, and therefore think it necessary to patronize a high-priced tailor in order to obtain clothing suited to their discriminating (?) taste, the great majority of the people appreciate the folly of "paying for a name" and place their orders with those dealers who only ask a fair profit on the goods handled. No one more truly representative of this latter class, could be pointed out than Mr. George H. Babcock, for although he caters to all classes of trade and is prepared to supply anything in the line of dependable clothing, he is content with a small margin of profit on all the many grades in which he deals. Mr. Babcock is a native of Newport, and began operations in Westerly on Broad street, in 1886, removing to his present commodious store, Nos. 16 and 18 Main street, in 1888. The premises are 38x62 feet in dimensions, and contain a very large stock, comprising clothing, hats and caps, gents'

Mrs. H. D. Burdick, Dealer in Fashionable Millinery and Art Fancy Goods of every description. Stamping done on any material promptly and satisfactorily. No. 24 Main St., Westerly.—Good taste in dress is unfortunately not possessed by every one, but good judgment concerning the most advantageous establishment to patronize is a more common faculty and can in a great measure replace the first-named gift. For instance, many ladies who appreciate the help afforded by able and experienced assistance in the choosing and trimming of hats, etc., make a practice of obtaining all their millinery goods at the establishment conducted by Mrs. H. D. Burdick, at 24 Main St., and the results attained are flattering alike to that lady's good taste and to the sound discrimination of those who avail themselves of her facilities. Mrs. Burdick deals largely in fashionable millinery and art fancy goods of every discription, her stock being a most attractive one and including the latest and most successful novelty. Stamping on any material is promptly and satisfactorily done. Particular attention is given to orders for millinery work, and out of town orders are solicited, commissions being executed at short notice and at extremely reasonable rates, care being taken to suit the individuality of the purchaser.

are prepared to quote the lowest market rates. He also carries a full line of Special fine "Paillard" Non-Magnetic and Waltham Non-Magnetic Watches. Standard time is wired daily. Telephone connections to all parts. Office of Postal Telegraph Cable Co. Employment is given to three assistants, and a specialty is made of Repairing at moderate rates. The "Lodge" Lever Clock Gold Gilt Front, Nickel Plated Frame with Glass in sides, is put up as 1 Day Time, 1 Day Time and Alarm and 1 Day Strike. The alarm runs an unusual length of time, making them very desirable for heavy sleepers, while the clock as above stated can be had with or without alarm, and with or without strike. This clock is one of the many Nickeled Novelties put on the market by the justly celebrated Seth Thomas Clock Co.

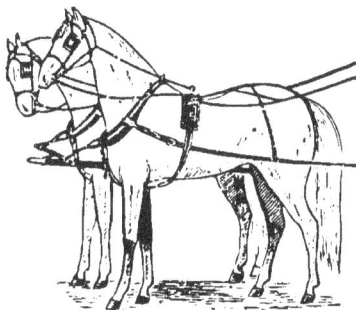

E. N. Denison & Co. Jewelers and Silversmiths, Full line of Watches, Clocks, etc. Dealers in Honest and Warrantable Goods, Finest Repairing at Fair Prices, Westerly, R. I. —Buying Jewelry, Silver Ware, Watches or anything in that line of any unknown dealer is very much like investing in a lottery, the main difference being that a lottery may possibly return much more than was put in, while the dealer will surely not give you *more* than your money's worth and experience shows that the chances are you will get less. As these facts are generally understood, it is perfectly natural that a large proportion of the residents of Westerly and vicinity should buy the major part of their Jewelry etc., at the establishment conducted by Messrs. E. N. Denison & Co. at No. 50 High Street, for this has been in existence so long and has made so honorable a record that customers rightly feel a positive assurance that both goods and prices will prove just as they should be. The business was founded many years ago by Mr. Thomas Perry, who was succeeded in 1861 by Mr. John S. Fifield, this gentleman giving place in 1871 to Messrs. Denison & Fifield, and the present firm-name being adopted in 1873. Mr. E. N. Denison is a native of Stonington, Conn., and is personally one of the best known of our local merchants. He gives his business very careful attention and takes pride in maintaining the enviable reputation so long connected with it. The store is 15x58 feet in dimensions, and the stock is exceptionally varied, being complete in every department and embracing nothing but honest and warrantable goods, Jewelry, Silverware, Watches, Clocks etc., comprising the latest novelties as well as full lines of staple designs, which are always on hand to choose from, and we need hardly say the firm

The Westerly Harness and Leather Store, Geo. A. Champlin Proprietor. 44 Main Street. Opp. Stone Mill, Westerly, R. I.—The advantages of using a strong, honestly-made and well-proportioned harness, are many and not the least important of them is the safety one gains by so doing. A cheap harness may do very well under ordinary circumstances, although we dispute even this point, but when any great and sudden strain comes upon it. When your horse jumps at the report of a firearm, the whistle of a locomotive, the clang of a factory bell, something is apt to give way and somebody is liable to get hurt. The well-made harness is durable handsome and soft, and is by far the cheaper in the long run. No one that we know of is better prepared to furnish his customers with a harness that they can safely depend upon under all circumstances than Mr. Geo. A. Champlin proprietor of the Westerly Harness and Leather Store located at No. 44 Main Street, opposite the Stone Mill, and since he began operations in 1887, he has built up a reputation of which he has good reason to be proud, for good work, fair prices, and general square dealing. Mr. Champlin was born in Westerly and has a large circle of friends in this vicinity. A store measuring 15x60 feet. is occupied, and stocked with a large and varied assortment of Harnesses, Whips, Horse Blankets, Robes, Surcingles, Carriage Mats, Brushes, Combs, Harness Oil, Axle Oil, Feed Bags and all kinds of Harness Trimmings, Harness Leather, Sole Leather, Lace Leather and Belting in all widths. Order work and repairing is given prompt and careful attention.   2

Maxson's Sons, Successors to C. Maxson & Co. Hardware, Paints, Oils, Novelties, Iron, Steel, Glass, Builders', Mechanics' and Blacksmiths' supplies; Shoe Thread and Nails; Stone Cutters' Tools; Marine Hardware; Job Lots, Sheet Lead and Pipe; Pumps, Oars and Rope. Westerly, R. I.—There are but few business undertakings in this or any other community which have been carried on for nearly half a century, and when one of such long standing is found, the natural presumption is that it possesses special claims on the patronage of the public. For this reason, the enterprise conducted by "Maxson's Sons" is deserving of prominent mention in a review of Westerly's representative mercantile undertakings, for it was founded in 1843 and has been successfully continued ever since, coming under the control of the present firm in 1881. The proprietors are Messrs. A. W. and C. A. Maxson, the former being a native of Stonington. Conn., and the latter of New York state. A very extensive trade is done in Hardware, Paints, Oils, etc., and a very heavy stock is on hand to choose from, comprising Iron, Steel and Glass, Builders', Mechanics' and Blacksmiths' supplies; Shoe Thread and Nails, Stone Cutters' Tools; Marine Hardware; Sheet Lead and Pipe; Pumps, Oars, Rope. etc., novelties and all goods not kept elsewhere, artistic brass goods, Cabinet Hardware, Blasting and Sporting Powder, Shot and Fuse. Two floors and a basement, of the dimensions of 15x60 feet are occupied, and sufficient assistance is employed to ensure the prompt and accurate filling of all orders. This house has a more than local reputation for supplying dependable goods at bottom prices, and are in a position to easily meet all honorable competitors.

———

H. G. York, Dealer in Cut Flowers and Flowering Plants, also Groceries. Greenhouse, Elm street, Westerly, R. I.—This is neither the time nor the place to indulge in a eulogy of flowers and flower lovers, and indeed it is very unprofitable work at the best to endeavor to argue people into a fondness for and appreciation of these "smiles of nature" as somebody has called them, for if a person has not a love for flowers born in him, it is idle to seek to inculcate it by example or precept. In this article then we will treat the subject from its commercial side alone, and that this is of great importance, no one need be told who is t all familiar with the demands of custom and fashion as regards flowers and their uses. To begin with it is impossible to conceive of articles better adapted to all occasions than are flowers for taste and custom sanction their use in time of joy and in time of sorrow, on the breast of the bride and on the bosom of the departed one. Flowers may be safely given when other gifts would be refused, and so wide is the range of their capabilities that either distant respect or present admiration may be expressed by them more eloquently than words. In Westerly, the trade in cut flowers and flowering plants is extensively conducted by Mr. H. G. York; his green-houses are located on Elm street, and cover an area of 27 by 92 feet, of ground and his skill and facilities are such as to render competition out of the question. Mr. York is a native of Westerly and has been engaged in the grocery business in this town for about twenty years, and now runs a meat cart, and deals some in groceries, in addition to his flower business, which he established in 1889. Mr. York furnishes anything in his line at the lowest rates, and is prompt in the delivery of all orders.

———

H. B. Gavitt, Dealer in Household Furniture of all descriptions, Bedding, etc.; 35 and 37 West Broad street. Westerly.—It is no secret that much of the household furniture in the market is made simply to sell, and has no wearing qualities, and it is also generally known that it is practically impossible for anyone not an expert to judge between the reliable and the unreliable, for paint, varnish and glue will do wonders in covering up defects, and only practical use will expose them. Now, we have not the least idea of declaring that Mr. H. B Gavitt is the only trustworthy dealer in furniture in this vicinity, and he himself would be the first to deny such a statement; but we are confident that he is prepared to offer as much value for money paid as anyone in the business, and therefore we cordially recommend his establishment to our readers. It is located at Nos. 35 and 37 West Broad street, and comprises one floor of the dimensions of 25 x 70 feet; 2 floors measuring 45 x 70 feet, and a basement (used as a workshop) 25 x 70 feet in size. An immense stock of household furniture. bedding, etc., of all descriptons is at hand to choose from, and bottom prices rule in every department. Every facility is at hand for the finishing and repairing of furniture, and employment is given to 4 competent assistants. This business was founded many years ago, and came under the control of Messrs. Hazzard & Gavitt in 1868. this firm being succeeded by Messrs. H. B. Gavitt & Co. in 1873, and the present proprietor assuming sole control in 1878. He is a native of Westerly, and is widely known here as a business man of integrity and enterprise, who makes no representations not fully warranted by the facts.

C. H. Holdredge, Manufacturer and Repairer of Carriages and Wagons of all kinds; all kinds of Harness, Whips, Robes, Blankets, Harness Oil, Axle Oil and Grease; Carriage Trimming and Carriage Blacksmithing; Main St., Westerly.—The best of stock is none too good to put into carriages and wagons that are made to "wear well" as well as to "look well," and it is largely owing to his appreciation of this fact, and of his acting accordingly when filling orders, that Mr. C. H. Holdredge enjoys the high reputation he has so long held in connection with the manufacturing and repairing of carriages and wagons of every description. He was born in Montville, Ct., and served in the army during the Rebellion, being at the present time Commander of the local Grand Army Post. He has been identified with his present line of business for over a score of years, having begun operations in 1867. The premises made use of are located at 101 Main street, and comprise a workshop measuring 30 x 76 feet; and a repository, of the dimensions of 32 x 100 feet. The shop is fitted up with improved machinery, run by steam power, and employment is given to from six to eight assistants, carriages and wagons being made to order at short notice, and at the lowest prices consistent with the use of selected materials and the employment of skilled labor. Carriage blacksmithing, trimming and repairing in general is done in first-class style, and no trouble is spared to deliver all orders promptly when promised. Mr. Holdredge carries a very extensive and varied stock of carriages, harness, whips, robes, blankets, harness oil, axle oil and grease, etc.; and those wishing anything in this line may save money, time and trouble by giving him a call, as his prices are always low and every article is fully guaranteed to prove as

represented. Mr. Holdredge is also the manufacturer of Burch's Patent Gear, a new invention for wagons and carriages, which renders the vehicle very easy to ride in; and the King bolt, one setting back of center enabling one to turn in a smaller space than with any other gear. There is also a sand band with every gear to protect it from dust and dirt.

W. H. Green, Carriage and Wagon Painting and Lettering, at C. H. Holdredge's Carriage Repository, Main street, Westerly, R. I.—Not only the appearance but the durability of a vehicle is dependent upon the manner in which it is painted, and those who think to save money by letting the wagons or carriages go uncared for in this respect, make a great mistake. Carriage painting is a business by itself, and in order to be sure of attaining the best results, it is necessary to place orders with one who makes a specialty of such work, and has both the facilities and the experience to enable him to guarantee satisfaction to the most critical. Such a man is Mr. W. H. Green, doing business at Mr. C. H. Holdredge's carriage repository, Main street, and we take pleasure in recommending him to our readers, for those who have had dealings with him speak in the highest terms of his skill and reliablity. He is a native of New Haven, Ct., and has carried on his present enterprise since 1880, having at that time succeeded Mr. Chas. Darling who had been in control since 1876. Mr. Green utilizes premises of the dimensions of 32x80 feet and employs two efficient assistants, thus being in a position to fill orders at short notice. Carriage and wagon painting, and lettering will be done in a thoroughly workmanlike manner at moderate rates, carefully selected stock being used, and the durability as well as the beauty of the work being given painstaking consideration.

Mrs. N. Pierce, Dealer in French Millinery, Trimmed and Untrimmed Hats, Ribbons, Velvets, Feathers, Flowers, and everything used in the millinery line. 41 Broad street, Westerly, R. I.—Such a stock as is carried by Mrs. N. Pierce, doing business at No. 41 Broad street, is not to be described in detail, first, because it is so extensive and varied that pages would be taken up in an attempt to do so, and second, because it is being added to so constantly that no description would hold good for any length of time. Therefore the best advice we can give our readers is to visit the establishment and see for themselves, and they will be well repaid for doing so, as the assortment of French millinery, trimmings, etc., comprises the very latest fashionable novelties in these lines and is worthy of the most careful inspection. Mrs. Pierce is a native of this state, and inaugurated her present enterprise in 1873. Her experience and taste enable her to satisfy the most fastidious in the doing of custom work, and the employment of two skilful assistants during the season assures the prompt filling of all orders. Trimmed and untrimmed hats and bonnets, ribbons, velvets, feathers, ornaments, flowers, etc., are offered in great variety, and the prices quoted will bear the severest comparison with those named anywhere on articles of similar grade.

Job Thorp, Tinner, and Dealer in Stoves, House-furnishing Goods, etc., No. 40 West Broad street, Westerly, R. I.—Experienced housekeepers do not need to be told that a first-class cook-stove or range is the cheapest as well as the most convenient to use, but those who are about to "set up housekeeping" and want to be as economical as possible are very apt to buy an inferior cook-stove because it is cheaper than one combining all the modern improvements and they think it will be "good enough for a small family." This is a mistake, for an inferior stove is wasteful of fuel, is hard to regulate as regards the disposal of the heat, and will prove a constant cause of annoyance. A really first-class article can be bought for a moderate sum if the right store be patronized, and a call at the establishment of Mr. Job Thorp, at No. 40 West Broad St., will demonstrate the fact that he is prepared to quote bottom prices on stoves, stove furniture, etc., and to supply the latest and most successful novelties in this line. The premises comprise one floor and a basement, measuring 30x60 feet, and a well-equipped work-shop, and a large and well-selected stock is on hand, made up of cooking and heating stoves, tinware, crockery, and house furnishing goods in general. Mr. Thorp has carried on his present business since 1883. He has built up a large trade and employs four efficient assistants, tin-mithing and general jobbing being done at short notice and at moderate rates. All his goods are guaranteed to prove as represented, and customers can always depend upon receiving prompt and polite attention and getting full value for every dollar paid.

Bernard Halpin, Dealer in Groceries, Provisions, Flour, Teas, Coffees, Spices, Cigars, Tobacco. Canned Goods, Fruits in Season, &c., 64 West Broad street, Westerly, R. I.—The business carried on by Mr. Bernard Halpin at No. 64 West Broad St., was established by Messrs. Towomey & Malaghan, who were succeeded by the present proprietor in 1888. Mr. Halpin served in the army four years and has been connected with the school committee, and is so widely known here that extended personal mention is quite unnecessary. The stock carried is both abundant and varied, for it is made up of staple and fancy groceries, provisions. flour, etc., and is so complete in every department that all classes of trade can be successfully catered to. and every order can be filled at short notice. The premises in use measure 22 by 50 feet, and employment is given to two experienced and careful assistants. Especial attention should be called to the teas and coffees offered, for these goods are of exceptionally fine flavor and will be found satisfactory to the most fastidious. They are carefully selected from the most reliable sources, and are quoted at the very lowest market rates. The assortment of cigars, tobacco, fruit and canned goods is deserving of particular commendation, for not only is it large and complete, but is composed exclusively of the productions of producers whose reputations are beyond question, and while every article is fully warranted to prove as represented, no fancy prices are quoted.

R. Mitchell, Scotch and Domestic Bakery; Bread, Cake and Pastry; 82 Main Street, Westerly, R. I.—The popular establishment, located at No. 82 Main street, is well-called the "Scotch and domestic" bakery. for a specialty is made by its proprietor of supplying families, and the goods are of that even excellence that is so much appreciated by that class of trade. Mr. Mitchell is a native of Scotland, and inaugurated the enterprise alluded to in 1889. His success has been proportionate to his merits, and this is equivalent to saying that a business has been built up, equal to that of any similar establishment in Westerly. The premises occupied comprise one floor and a basement each 700 square feet in dimensions, and a very large assortment of bread, cake and pastry is at all times carried. Four thoroughly experienced assistants are employed, and an extensive wholesale and retail business is transacted. All orders for home-made bread. etc., will be executed at short notice. and filled and delivered accurately, while customers are served in a most polite and attentive manner.

National Phenix Bank, Broad Street, Westerly, R. I.—The policy of the National Phenix Bank has been so clearly defined during the more than 70 years that the institution has been in operation, that it would be merely a waste of space to describe it in detail, but in simple justice to the fidelity and ability with which the present management have maintained the time-honored reputation of the bank, we must say that home enterprises and local undertakings were never more sure of receiving discriminating but liberal aid than is now the case, and the manner in which the gentlemen constituting the officers and directors are identified with the manufacturing and commercial interests of Westerly, gives most excellent reason to believe that they are peculiarly well-fitted to discharge their responsible duties to the best possible advantage. The National Phenix Bank was incorporated as a state bank in 1818, and its re-organization under the national banking laws occurred in 1865. The added powers given by its present charter have been most wisely availed of, and the work done by the bank during the exceptionally trying period immediately succeeding the war, was of a character that firmly established the ability and patriotism of those having it in charge, and has by no means yet been forgotten by Westerly's representative business men. The bank has a capital of $150,000, and far from being dependent upon past usefulness for present patronage, is one of the most active and energetic financial institutions in the state. The best indication of what may reasonably be expected from it, is that afforded by the character of those acting as officers and directors, a list of whom is herewith given: President, Edwin Babcock; Cashier, J. B. Foster.

Directors.

Edwin Babcock,	Chas. P. Chapman,
J. B. Foster,	Franklin Metcalf,
Wm. A. Burdick,	Wm. Hoxsey,
Geo. M. Burdick,	Orlando R. Smith.

J. M. Pendleton & Co., Insurance Agents, Corner High and Broad Streets, Westerly, R. I. —From the very nature of things, it is impossible for even the most experienced business men to agree always upon what constitutes a fair business risk, but there are certain risks which are so foolishly hazardous as to condemn on prima-facie evidence the men who take them. There is certainly no excuse for a business man, carrying an ordinarily insurable stock, who will go on without such protection, for the amount saved per annum is so ridiculously small considering the chance of loss incurred, that there is practically no compensation whatever for the risk taken. As a matter of fact, very few merchants do allow their stock to remain unprotected deliberately, but policies will expire, and other details claim attention, so that the renewal is neglected almost unconsciously. For this and other reasons, the methods pursued at the old-established agency of Messrs. J. M. Pendleton & Co. are very popular with business men and the general public, for this concern are very careful of the interests of clients, and no policy issued through this office is allowed to lapse without due attention being called to the matter. The most reliable companies are represented, and the lowest attainable rates are quoted on "insurance that insures." This agency was founded by Mr. J. M. Pendleton, in 1860, and the existing firm-name has been had since 1888. The founder is dead, and the business is continued by Mr. C. A. Morgan, who is a native of Stonington, Ct., and is widely known in business circles. The agency is located at the corner of High and Broad Sts., and the character of the service provided will be best shown by the following list of companies represented:

Hartford Insurance Company of Hartford.
.Ætna   "   "   "   "
Phenix   "   "   "   "
Traveller's Life and Accident   "   "
Mutual Benefit Life of New Jersey.
Springfield Fire and Marine.
Glens Falls.
Ins. Co. of North America.
Fire Association of Phila.
Home Insurance Company of New York.
Continental   "   "   "
German American.
Royal.
Commercial Union.
City of London.
Lancashire.
Sun Fire Office.
Hamburg—Bremen.
Holyoke Mutual.
Franklin   "
Pawtucket   "
Merchants' and Farmers' Mutual.
Losses to amount of over $350,000 have been paid at this agency to entire satisfaction of assured.

J. H. Griffin, Dealer in Groceries, Meats, Fish and Vegetables, 55 West Broad Street, Westerly, R. I.—There is no doubt that the enterprise carried on by Mr. J. H. Griffin is entitled to a foremost position among the numerous undertakings of a similar nature to be found in this town, for it was originally founded by Mr. Charles R. Woodburn, who was succeeded by the present proprietor in 1889, and has been conducted in a manner that has secured for it a large and enduring patronage. The establishment, to which we have reference, is located at 55 West Broad street, and is of the dimensions of 18 by 60 feet, and is well stocked with an extensive assortment of goods, comprising groceries, meats, fish, etc. Mr. Griffin is, therefore, enabled to supply his customers with fresh and reliable goods at moderate rates. Two competent assistants are employed, and orders are promptly filled, and the delivery system is so perfect as to render mistakes or annoying delays almost impossible of occurrence. Mr. Griffin is a native of Charlestown, R. I., and served three years in the army during the Rebellion. He gives the various details of his business close and constant attention, and is ever on the alert to improve the service offered, the result being that no concern in this vicinity is more generally popular or in a position to hold out more genuine advantages to customers.

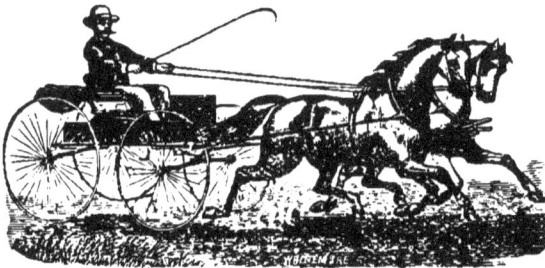

C. F. Rollinson, Livery, Hack, Boarding and Feed Stable. Carriages at Depot on arival of all trains. Terms reasonable; entrance, next Windsor House, 67 High street, Westerly, R. I.—There are none too many good stable in this section of the state, or indeed in any other of which we have knowledge, and for this reason we take pleasure in calling attention to the establishment carried on by Mr. C. F. Rollinson, at No. 67 High street, entrance next to the Windsor House, for a specialty is made of boarding and feeding horses here and animals are sure of receiving the best of care and an abundance of proper food. This stable has been open to the public for a number of years, but never had so high a reputation before, as it eas gained since coming into the possession of its present proprietor, in 1885, at which time the firm name was Rollinson & Co. In 1887, Mr. C. F. Rollinson assumed entire control of the business. He is a native of Woonsocket, R. I., and has many friends in Westerly and vicinity, and is considered an excellent judge of horse flesh, as indeed he should be, for he has had a great deal to do with horses, in one way and another, and knows from experience just how to handle them. This stable is very convenient, and is well arranged throughout. The charges for livery service, board or feed are very reasonable, and we can assure our readers that those who entrust their horses to Mr. Rollinson will have no reason to regret having done so, for they will be given the best of care at all times, and no trouble is spared to guarantee complete satisfaction to every customer.

C. F. Berry, Agent; Manufacturer of all kinds of Harness, and Dealer in Whips, Brushes, Oils, etc., etc.; 15 West Broad St., Westerly.—Now that so many horse-owners are giving more careful attention than ever before to the question of how their animals are shod, it would be well if they gave a little notice to the question of harness, also. So long as a horse is improperly harnessed, he cannot do his work as he should; and as few horses are capable of doing a great deal more than is required of them, it is well to aid them by all reasonable means. It takes experience to make a good harness, especially fitted for a certain animal, and few of our local manufacturers are so well prepared to undertake anything of this kind as is Mr. C. F. Berry, having a place of business on West Broad street. Mr. Berry is a native of Westerly, and succeeded Mr. C. W. Frazier in his business in 1888, and his reputa-

tion for turning out handsome and durable work is unsurpassed. Premises measuring 250 square feet are made use of, and employment is given to two competent assistants. Mr. Berry manufactures harness of all kinds to order, also repairing is done with neatness and despatch, and using only the best of stock, is enabled to guarantee the durability of his work. His prices are always reasonable, and will bear the severest comparison with those named anywhere on work of equal merit. A well selected assortment of whips, brushes, oils, etc., etc., is on hand to select from, and many useful articles may be obtained here.

Peoples Savings Bank, Westerly, R. I.— There are very few purely business enterprises which work such great benefit to the community at large as do Savings Banks, and the lasting good derived from the operations of these institutions, as distinguished from the temporary help given by charitable undertakings, is due simply to the fact that the one encourages the people to help themselves, while the other is apt to bring about a feeling of dependence upon outside aid. It is far better for the individual and for society to induce a man to save a dollar than to give him five times that sum, and certainly no stronger inducement to save can be offered than that afforded by the surety that every dollar put away will be forthcoming when wanted, and that the depositor will be assisted by as liberal a rate of interest as circumstances will allow. For these and similar reasons, it seems to us as though too general and liberal support could not be given to the Peoples Savings Bank, incorporated in 1886, and we are happy to say that we are evidently by no means alone in this belief, for despite the comparatively recent origin of the institution in question, the facilities offered have already been very largely availed of. The Peoples Savings Bank is most appropriately named, and the community would do well to bear in mind the fact that on the people depends the measure of usefulness it is capable of exerting. The incorporators have provided a place in which savings may be deposited, they have satisfied the proper authorities as to their fitness and responsibility and have bound themselves to administer the affairs of the bank with due regard to all legal restrictions, while their standing in the community affords even more convincing security that all legal and moral obligations will be faithfully discharged. Having done these things, they have reason to confidentially expect the co-operation of the people, and there can be no doubt but that such co operation will be readily and heartily given. The officers of the bank are so widely and favorably known in financial and mercantile circles that the following list of names will be accepted as the best possible evidence that the institution could not be in better

George W. Foster.

Dealer in Daily and Weekly Newspapers, Magazines, Periodicals, Cheap Publications, Blank and Pass Books, Tobacco and Cigars; Subscriptions received, Orders promptly attended to; In Leonard House, 63 Main St., and 21 Broad St., Westerly. —The establishment carried on by Mr. George W. Foster, in Westerly, and located at Nos. 21 Broad street and 63 Main street, are most attractive places to visit, for they contain very large and tastefully selected stocks, including all the daily and weekly newspapers, magazines, periodicals, cheap publications, blank and pass books, and a fine line of tobacco and cigars, including the best brands. Those who possess literary tastes will find a call will prove both agreeable and profitable, for the goods are displayed to excellent advantage, and the prices quoted are exceptionally moderate. Mr. Foster is almost universally known hereabouts, having carried on his present line of business since 1865, purchasing the stock of Mr. Edward Chapman, who succeeded Elisha Barnes, the original founder, in 1849. He is a native of Providence, R. I., and served four years in the army during the Rebellion, and was discharged as Orderly Sergeant. Employment is given to a competent force of assistants, and every customer may depend upon receiving prompt and polite attention. Mr. Foster makes a specialty of all the leading magazines and periodicals, and subscriptions received for the same are promptly attended to, and those purchasing anything handled by Mr. Foster are sure of getting an equivalent for their money in every instance.

J. E. Sheffield.

Tin, Zinc, Copper and Sheet Iron Worker; Tin Roofing a Specialty: Westerly, R. I.—There is no builder or housekeeper but what often has occasion for the services of a competent tin and sheet iron worker, and in this connection, it is fitting to say that it is the poorest possible economy to to have "cheap" tin or copper work done. It is the most expensive in the long run. The best plan is to visit such an establishment as that conducted by Mr. J. E. Sheffield, on Mechanic st., who has been located here since 1885, but has always lived in Westerly where he learned his trade. He handles stove-pipes, gutters, conductors, &c. and does pump and lead pipe work and tin roofing, and guarantees it to give entire satisfaction, while his prices are very reasonable. Order work in plumbing for houses and stores; Also, cement drain pipes laid, and all work done at short notice in a superior manner. Every facility is at hand for repairing roofs, conductors of all kinds and general jobbing, and moderate charges are made in every instance.

The Crefeld Mills,

Westerly, R. I.—Retail buyers, as a general thing, depend more on the reputation of the firm with which they deal than on the standing of the manufacturers whose goods they handle, and while this practice has its advantages, it also has its drawbacks; and prominent among these latter, is the difficulty of giving "honor where honor is due" when goods prove exceptionally satisfactory. For instance, one might purchase some of the Crefeld Mills shirtings at retail, without having the least idea of who the manufacturers were, and, as a natural consequence, should anyone note the excellence of the fabric and inquire the name of the maker, the best that could be done would be to refer the inquirer to the dealer patronized. We make special mention of the Crefeld Mills, as it is undeniable that this concern are sparing no pains to produce the most reliable and desirable shirtings possible. A magnificent plant is utilized, over 340 looms and 10,500 spindles being operated, and no establishment in the country is better qualified to attain satisfactory results. The present name was adopted in 1888, the enterprise having been formerly conducted by the Moss Manufacturing Company; and the magnitude of operations as now carried on is indicated by the employment of 200 assistants, and the production of 50,000 yards per week. Many leading business men are identified with the enterprise, and the position of president is held by Mr. Charles O. Read, Mr. W. Maxwell Greene acting as treasurer, and Mr. F. H. Potter as agent.

W. A. Burk.

Hack, Livery and Boarding Stable: Carriages at the depot on arrival of all trains: rear of Leonard House, Westerly. —Although it is undoubtedly difficult if not impossible to carry on a livery stable (or any other enterprise) so as to satisfy everybody, still, as a general thing, the public are not slow to appreciate liberal and honorable dealing, and show their appreciation by the support they give to establishments conducted in accordance with such methods. A case in point is that afforded by the livery and boarding stable of which Mr. W. A. Burk is the proprietor, for during the twelve years which this gentleman has carried on the establishment in question, a gratifying trade has been built up which is steadily increasing. Mr. Burk has some very desirable teams for livery service, and those who wish to hire a good horse and a stylish, easy running carriage for a moderate sum would do well to give him a call. Orders are filled at very short notice, and the teams are kept in such first-class condition as to be presentable in any company. Quite an extensive Hack and Boarding business is done, for Mr. Burk has good accommodations for horses. He employs two competent assistants, and every animal left in the care of his stable will receive the best of treatment. The stable in question is located in the rear of Leonard House, carriages from which are at the depot on arrival of all trains. Mr. Burk is a native of Hopkinton, R. I., and those dealing with him may safely depend upon getting the full worth of their money every time.

The Buffum Loan & Trust Co., Successors to F. C. & E. H. Buffum; Established 1880;

Incorporated 1888; Capital Stock, $200,000; Capital paid in, $100,500; Surplus and Undivided Profits, $15,721. Office open July 1st to Oct. 1st. Loans pay 7 per cent. Guaranteed or 8 per cent. not Guaranteed. No investor has ever foreclosed a mortgage or lost a cent in any manner whatever. Never loan exceeding ⅓ of actual cash value; Westerly, R. I.—The Buffum Loan and Trust Company holds a leading position among those corporations which have for their chief aim the development of the "New South," and its record since its organization has been such as to amply justify those who predicted the highest success for the enterprise, founding their prophecy on the demand existing for such an undertaking, and the character and ability of the men having it in charge. The company was formed for the purpose of making and negotiating loans on real estate, and its business includes the handling of securities in general, the reception on deposit of moneys from individuals, corporations, etc., and, in short, the discharge of all the usual functions of a loan and trust company. The articles of incorporation are very carefully framed, and are evidently designed to protect the interests of all parties concerned, a notable clause being that providing that the highest amount of indebtedness to which the company can subject itself shall not exceed the capital stock subscribed and paid in. The statement showing the financial condition of the corporation, issued at the close of the second six months' business, May 31, 1889, is worthy of the careful attention of every investor, and an idea of its character may be gained from the fact that a semi-annual dividend of 3½ per cent. was made, payable on and after June 5th, 1889, in addition to carrying $15,000 to the surplus fund. Officers and directors are all resident in Florida, with the exception of Mr. Franklin Metcalf, of Carolina, R. I., and the company's success is largely due to their intimate and personal knowledge of Southern property and resources. A branch office is maintained on West Broad St., Westerly (on the Bridge), and callers will be given all desired information, and afforded every facility to ascertain what has been done in the past and what may be effected in the future. The following is a full list of those actively concerned in the management of affairs:—
FREDERICK C. BUFFUM, President; EDWARD H. BUFFUM, Vice President and Auditor; CLAUDE E. CONNOR, Secretary and Treasurer.

FINANCE COMMITTEE.

Frederick C. Buffum, Edward H. Buffum and Samuel W. Teague.

BOARD OF DIRECTORS.

Frederick C. Buffum, Stanton, Florida; Edward H. Buffum, Stanton, Florida; Claude E. Connor, Ocala, Florida; Horace L. Cilley, South Lake Weir, Florida; Robert L. Anderson, Ocala, Florida; Franklin Metcalf, Carolina, Rhode Island; Samuel W. Teague, Lady Lake, Florida.

Pawcatuck National Bank, Westerly, R. I.—The past forty years have brought about

so many and such radical changes in manufacturing and mercantile methods, that it is obvious that a financial institution which has been steadily conducted throughout that period, and has passed through all the "panics" and business revolutions occurring during that time, not only without impairment of its credit but with a steady gain in the confidence of the public, must have been exceptionally fortunate in the ability and character of its management. Such is the record held by the Pawcatuck National Bank, and it is gratifying to be able to state that this time-honored institution was never better prepared to continue its good work than it is at the present time. It holds a very high position among our New England Banks, and its facilities for the carrying on of a general banking business are so complete and reliable that it is natural they should be in great request among local business men. Very favorable relations are enjoyed with other banks throughout the country, and for correspondents the Pawcatuck has the two leading institutions in their respective cities—the National Park Bank, of New York and the Maverick National Bank, of Boston. The Pawcatuck Bank was incorporated in 1849, and was re-organized under the national banking laws in 1865. It has a capital of $100,000, and its present financial condition, taken in connection with its standing in the business community, reflects great credit on those having its interests in charge. The President is Mr. Peleg Clark, the Cashier, Mr. J. A. Brown, and the Board of Directors is made up of the following well-known citizens:
Peleg Clark.   P. S. Barber,
Charles H. Hinckley, Stanton Hazard,
C. B. Cottrell, Jr.

C. D. Crandall & Son, Painting, Graining,

Kalsomining, Wall Tinting, Paper Hanging and Interior Decorating in all their branches, done promptly and in a workmanlike manner. Shop, corner West Broad and Mechanic streets, Westerly.—New England has so much "weather" to the square inch, that anything that is to be exposed to its influence should be particularly tough and hardy,and this is especially the case with house paints, as on their durability not only the appearance, but much of the preservation of the structure depends. Messrs. C. B. Crandall & Son, of West Broad street, have gained an enviable reputation for furnishing the best stock and applying it in the most thorough manner, and all orders for house or sign painting will be filled at short notice and in a perfectly satisfactory style. This business has rapidly and steadily increased since its incorporation. Messrs. Crandall & Son are prepared to fill orders for anything in the house and sign painting line at short notice and also carry a heavy and varied stock of paints, oils and varnishes. They employ only skilled workmen and give close personal attention to every order received, and in all departments of their business unusually low prices prevail.

F. C. Buffum, Florida Lemon Groves, Westerly, R. I.—Persons, who can spare from their incomes from $20.00 per quarter, and upwards, are invited to examine this letter and the offer made herewith. The planting of lemon groves in Florida offers to the investor, at the present time, one of the best opportunities for profit that can be found in any field of investment.

First:—The fruit is not a luxury, but a necessity. The demand for it increases out of all proportion to the increase of the population. From a report just received from the U. S. Inspector of Customs, it is shown that during the last four years the consumption of lemons has increased over a quarter of a million boxes per annum. A large part of this increase is due to its extended use for culinary and medicinal purposes.

Second:—The crop of lemons raised at present in this country is so small in comparison with the immense quantity of foreign fruit sold here as to be almost represented by zero. There is no doubt but a great industry in Florida lemon raising is bound to spring up, as portions of this state are the only sections of this country fitted for the successful culture of the fruit. The growers, who enter the field now, in the infancy of the industry, will reap the heaviest reward.

Third:—The Florida Villa Franca lemon is admitted to be the best lemon known to the trade, as the following letter, a sample of those received by Florida lemon-growers, will testify:—

219 So. WATER ST., CHICAGO, JULY 15, 1887.
E. L. CARNEY, LAKE WEIR, FLA.,

Dear Sir:—We wish to say that the lemons that you ship us give better satisfaction to the trade than any that we have ever handled. They run even, are firm, thin skinned, very juicy and of fine flavor.

We never saw them excelled.

All who tried them bought more and would have no others as long as they lasted. We hope that you may be able to raise them in such quantities as to supply the trade. We think they will drive the foreign fruit from our market.

Respectfully,   T. D. RANDALL & CO.

Fourth:—The best reason of all, is the convincing one of practical demonstration. The few growers, who are the fortunate owners of Florida lemon groves, are realizing large yearly profits therefrom. The returns of our Lake Weir groves were from $3.00 to $4.00 per box net or a profit of $800 to $1000 per acre. The groves, which yielded these returns, vary in age from five to eight years. I shall be glad to furnish the names of these grove owners to any one interested.

Their faith is shown by their works, as they are all increasing their lemon interest by planting more trees. I am one of this number, and am intending to increase my own acreage next winter. Should not know where to turn for an investment of equal profit. I have under my care nearly 300 acres of orange and lemon trees owned by different parties, in tracts of from five to twenty acres.

I have also the refusal, for another grove, of forty acres of land at a low price. This land is suitable for lemon culture and very desirably located, being on the south-east side of Lake Weir, elevated 100 feet above it, and one half mile from the R. R. Station. I am enabled by the co-operative plan, which has given entire satisfaction to the owners of the other groves, to plant, care for, and bring into bearing a grove of one acre at as low a price per acre as would be charged for a grove of 50 acres. The 40 acres, which I propose planting, will be under one fence and cultivated as a single grove, but each investor will hold a deed to own and control his own tract, whether one, five, or ten acres. My work is done on such a large scale that I can cultivate a grove more cheaply than an individual can take care of a single grove for himself. The prices for land, clearing, removing all stumps and roots, planting, care and cultivation are as low as is consistent with thorough good work.

COST OF AN ACRE GROVE.

Price of land	$ 30.00
Clearing land, removing all stumps and roots, fencing, plowing, setting 70 Villa Franca lemon trees, fertilizing and caring for same, one year . .	$125.00

This first year's expense is payable $38.75 quarterly. The trees are warranted to be living and in a healthy vigorous condition at the end of the first year. The annual cost of cultivation and care, each year, to the end of the fifth year is $40.00 per year payable $10.00 quarterly.

Total cost of three years' cultivation,	$120.00
	$275.00

The above figures do not cover the expense of gathering and shipping the fruit. At the end of the fourth year a grove will cost $275.00 and will be in bearing. Lemon groves from five to eight years of age cannot be bought for three times this cost, as the income from them is large. A very conservative estimate of the income to be derived from a lemon grove is:—

For the fifth year		$100 per acre.
" " sixth "	. . . . .	$200 " "
" " seventh "	. . . . .	$350 " "
" " eighth "	. . . . .	$500 " "

Gillett Bros., Snook Bros., E. L. Carney, C. L. Porter and others have realized much better figures than the above from their groves. T. B. Snook sold from 250 lemon trees at the age of eight years over $2000 worth of fruit. Actual results more than justify my figures. When a man has insured his life, and knows that in case of his death, a few thousand dollars will be paid to those that he leaves behind, he feels that he has done a good thing, and he has. But he must die to win. By investing in a Florida lemon grove, at the end of four short years the premiums are stopped, and a constantly increasing income is realized; or, if the owner of but a single acre grove dies before his property has been brought to a paying condition, his heirs will receive, annually, a sum perhaps as large as would be paid at one time by a Life Insurance Company.

Respectfully,   F. C. BUFFUM.

Mrs. J. G. Eells, Dress Making and Millinery Parlors; Ladies' Furnishings; Potter Building, Westerly, R. I.—All of our lady readers can doubtless call to mind instances which have come under their observation where the most costly costumes, made from the richest and most fashionable materials, utterly failed to produce a desirable effect by reason of the incompetency or carelessness of those who were entrusted with their making. The handsomest and most tasteful fabrics may easily be rendered quite unattractive by improper treatment, and the advantages to be gained by making use of the services of an experienced and skilful dressmaker, are too evident to render it necessary for us to dwell upon the importance of securing such aid. It is the general verdict among the ladies of Westerly and vicinity, who have examined specimens of the work done at the establishment of Mrs. J. G. Eells, that the results there attained are exceptionally satisfactory, and there has been ample time to form a competent judgment regarding the matter in question, for Mrs. Eells began operations in 1880, and her business has since rapidly and steadily developed, it now being the most extensive of the kind in town. Fine millinery is also largely dealt in, and order work is assured prompt and satisfactory attention, employment being given to 10 efficient assistants during the season. The dress making and millinery parlors are located in Potter block, the premises being 20 x 65 feet in dimensions, and supplied with the most improved facilities. A large stock of millinery goods and ladies' furnishings, embracing the very latest fashionable novelties, is always on hand to select from, and the prices quoted are uniformly moderate.

C. W. Brown, Coal and Wood, West Broad Street, Westerly, R. I.—It requires no small amount of experience to enable one to burn coal to the best advantage, even in an ordinary stove, and we may say in passing that some stoves are so very "ordinary" that they waste more than their cost in fuel every year. But even the best stove will not give entire satisfaction unless it is properly managed, and a good many of the complaints, which are heard regarding the quality of the coal furnished nowadays, are due to the carelessness or incompetence of those who use it. Some stoves work best with small or "nut" coal, others require a large size, and all need to be kept free from ashes or clinkers in order to burn coal economically. There is, of course, a good deal of difference in the quality of the various brands of coal on the market, but if the purchaser will patronize a reputable dealer, who handles all the standard varieties, he may be sure of getting a satisfactory article. Such a dealer is Mr. C. W. Brown, doing business on West Broad street, and as his facilities are strictly first-class, it follows that he is prepared to furnish anything in his line at the lowest market rates, and at very short notice. Mr. Brown does an extensive business in coal and wood, employs a sufficient force of assistants, and has a 100 foot dock, and enjoys an unsurpassed reputation for filling orders promptly, and for supplying strictly reliable goods at bottom prices.

Lyman Kenyon, Dealer in Groceries, Provisions, Flour, Canned Goods of All Kinds, Kerosene Oil; 72 Main Street, Westerly, R. I.—The reputation attained by the establishment conducted by Mr. Lyman Kenyon, at No. 72 Main st., proves it to be worthy of prominent mention in a review of the business enterprises of this vicinity, and has resulted in the building up of a large and desirable trade. Mr. Kenyon was born in Richmond, R. I., and began operations in Westerly in 1883. He utilizes premises having an area of 1000 square feet, and carries a very large, varied and carefully selected stock, for he caters to all tastes, and is prepared to furnish anything in the line of groceries and provisions at the lowest market rates. The most popular brands of flour are always to be had here in quantities to suit, low prices being quoted both on bag and barrel lots, and the goods being fully warranted to prove as represented. A fine assortment of canned goods is also carried, and as Mr. Kenyon only handles the productions of the most reputable packers, his customers are protected from the danger which experience has shown, attends the use of inferior articles of this kind. The stock of teas, coffees, spices, table condiments, relishes, etc., is exceptionally complete, and comprises goods that cannot fail to suit the most fastidious. A very popular characteristic of the management is the promptness with which all callers are attended to, for employment is given to 3 competent assistants, and all orders, large or small, can thus be given immediate and satisfactory attention.

Howe & Carr, Druggists, Cor. Main and Broad Streets, Westerly, R. I.—The pharmacy carried on by Messrs. Howe & Carr at the corner of Main and Broad sts., has gained an enviable reputation since it was opened in 1888, and in fact holds a leading position among the representative establishments of the kind in this section. Such a measure of success, gained in so short a time comparatively speaking, is exceptional perhaps, but it is nevertheless natural in the present case, for the firm had been engaged in a similar line of business in Providence for some 8 or 9 years, and were consequently well-prepared to conduct a thoroughly reliable pharmacy from the beginning. The Providence store is still maintained, there being 5 assistants employed there and 3 in Westerly. Mr. F. M. Howe has been sole proprietor of both establishments since the death of Mr. Carr, but the old firm-name is still continued. The premises occupied here are 30 feet square, and contain a very complete assortment of drugs, medicines and chemicals, as well as every facility for the compounding of prescriptions, this being the most important department of the business, and special pains being taken to carry it on to the best possible advantage. Orders are filled without delay, and every precaution is exercised to ensure absolute accuracy in every detail of the work. Toilet and fancy articles, soda and confectionery are quite largely dealt in, as are also paints, oils and artists' materials, and moderate prices are quoted in every branch of the business.

The Stillman Carriage Co., Manufacturers of One and Two Seat Carriages, Light and Heavy Farm Wagons of All kinds and Descriptions, Manufacturers of Stillman's Axle Oil,—the Best Axle Oil in the World; Coggswell Street, next to Express Office, Westerly. R. I.—There are many users of carriages and wagons who appreciate the fact that the reputation of the maker is the best guarantee that the purchaser of such a vehicle can have that he is getting the full worth of his money. The name of "Stillman" has long been widely and favorably known in connection with this branch of industry, and the Stillman Carriage Company, organized in 1887, has fully maintained the high reputation built up by Messrs. J. F. Stillman & Son, its predecessors. It is constituted of Messrs. E. F. and G. L. Stillman, both of whom were born in Westerly. The company manufacture one and two seat carriages, and light and heavy farm wagons of every description, maintaining an excellently-equipped shop and filling orders at short notice, and at the lowest prices consistent with the attainment of satisfactory results. The factory is two stories in height and 35 x 40 feet in dimensions, and there is a two-story repository of the dimensions of 30 x 50 feet, and 2 storehouses measuring 22 x 70 and 25 x 50 feet respectively. The premises are located on Coggswell st., next to the Express Office, and a fine stock of finished work is constantly on hand, callers being given every opportunity to make careful selection. Employment is given to 9 assistants, and vehicles will be made to order at short notice, while all kinds of repairing will be done in a thorough and workmanlike manner at moderate rates. The company manufacture Stillman's axle oil, which is considered to be the best axle oil in the market, and can supply it in quantities to suit at reasonable prices.

T. V. & V. C. Stillman, Machinists; Manufacturers of Paper Cutters and Wood Working Machinery; Shafting, Pulleys and Hangers to Order; Special Attention Given to Repairs; Westerly, R. I.—The enterprise carried on by Messrs. T. V. & V. C. Stillman, on West Broad st., had its inception nearly half a century ago, operations having been begun by Messrs. Stillman Bros.& Co. in 1843. This firm was succeeded by Messrs. H. S. Berry & Co., who gave place to Messrs. N. A. Woodward & Co. in 1876, the present proprietors assuming control in 1877. Both members of the firm are natives of Westerly, and are universally known here, Mr. T. V. Stillman having served as representative. A general machine business is carried on, the premises being of the dimensions of 50 x 75 feet, and being fitted up with improved machinery, run by water-power. The manufacture of paper cutters and wood-working machinery is quite extensively engaged in, and a specialty is made of the making of shafting, pulleys and hangers to order, employment being given to from 7 to 14 men, and commissions being executed at short notice and at moderate rates. Particular attention is given to repairing, and a more than local reputation is enjoyed in connection with this work, for the most difficult repairs are successfully undertaken, and orders are filled at the shortest possible notice, and at the lowest prices consistent with the attainment of the best results.

Philip H. Epie, Dealer in Ladies' and Gents' Underwear, Handkerchiefs, Notions, etc.; 71 Main street, Westerly.—Mr. Philip H. Epie only began business in Westerly in 1889, but his enterprise deserves mention in a review of that community's mercantile undertakings, from the fact that the proprietor is evidently determined to build up a prosperous trade, if the handling of dependable goods, the quoting of bottom prices and the assurance of equal courtesy and consideration to all can do it. He is a native of England and is thoroughly familiar with every detail of his business, being a close and discriminate buyer and giving his patrons a liberal share of the benefits he derives from his skill and care in this respect. The premises utilized have an area of 500 square feet, and are conveniently located at No. 71 Main street. The stock is new, fresh and attractive in every department, and includes a full selection of Ladies' and Gents' Underwear, Handkerchiefs, Notions, and many other articles, too numerous to mention. Should our readers wish anything in these lines, they would do well to give Mr. Epie a call, for he is prepared to quote prices as low as the lowest, and he guarantees every article as represented.

J. H. Doney, successor to N. F. Noyes, Marble and Granite worker, 103 Main street, Westerly, R. I. Monumental work in Marble, Granite and Freestone of every description. Cemetery and Lawn Vases, Marble and Slate Mantels. New designs and low prices. Satisfaction guaranteed. Correspondence solicited. —We can give no more useful and valuable advice to those wanting ornamental stone work of any kind done, than to counsel them to call at the establishment conducted by Mr. Joseph H. Doney, at No. 103 Main street, before placing their orders, for this gentleman is prepared to do Marble and Granite Work in a superior manner at moderate rates, and offers many novel and attractive designs to choose from. The business was formerly carried on by Mr. N. F. Noyes, who began operations in 1876, and was succeeded by Messrs. Doney & Davey in 1889, the present proprietor afterwards assuming sole control. He is a native of England, and has had long experience in his present line of industry, being thoroughly familiar with every detail. Monumental work in Marble, Granite and Freestone of every description will be done at very short notice, employment being given to from three to five assistants, and no pains being spared to deliver goods promptly when promised. Satisfaction is confidently guaranteed, and correspondence is solicited, estimates being cheerfully made and all desired information given on application. Cemetery and Lawn Vases and Marble and Slate Mantels are shown in many tasteful and attractive patterns, and the prices quoted will bear the severest examination and comparison.

A. S. Douglass. Livery, Hack and Express Stable. Carriages at Depot on Arrival of all Passenger Trains. A Fine Hack on Order. No. 6 Canal street, near Depot, Westerly.— There is one class of information that is ever fresh and always in demand in any town of any size, and that information pertains to Livery Stables, and where good ones may be found. One of the first impulses of the average well-to-do stranger in a place of any importance is to get a team and drive about, for in no other way can so accurate and complete a knowledge of the " lay of the land " be obtained in so short a time, in a manner which combines business and pleasure. That is, pleasure, if the turnout provided be such as pleasure can be taken in, for alas, in many cases it is the stranger, and not the pleasure, that is " taken in " when the team is hired. It is an axiom as true as any between the covers of an algebra, that good horses cannot be hired where good horses are not kept, and so it is of importance to " know the ropes,' and if you do so the probabilities are that when you want a nag you will make a call at the stable of which Mr. A. S. Douglass is the proprietor, located at No. 6 Canal street. The stable business was established by Mr. D. S. Douglass in 1855, and under his management attained a large patronage. The present proprietor assumed full control of the business in 1876. The premises cover an area of 20 by 90 feet, and contain a large number of first-class horses and carriages. This is a Livery, Hack and Express Stable. Carriages are in attendance at the Depot on arrival of all passenger trains, and orders for hacks or carriages for livery purposes, will receive prompt attention.

"The Bee Hive," Millinery, Fancy Goods. etc.; High and Broad Sts., Westerly.—It is a pleasure to make prominent and favorable mention of such an establishment as the "Bee Hive," located in Dixon House Square, at the corner of High and Broad Sts., for the motto of the management—"By Industry we thrive"—is particularly appropriate, insomuch as industry is unquestionably shown in providing the many attractions constantly being presented to patrons, and that the enterprise thrives on such a policy, is too evident to require demonstration. This undertaking was founded ten years ago, on Main St., but was removed, in 1888, to its present location, one of the most central in Westerly, and fronts on Broad and High Sts., one entrance opposite the Post Office, and is now conducted by Mr. J. Sterne, and there is no denying that he is "the right man in the right place," for the business is constantly increasing, and what is more, it is impossible to find a dissatisfied customer. Well, there is no reason why any one should be dissatisfied, for the stock is large, varied and fresh enough to suit all tastes, the prices are away down to the "lowest notch," the service is prompt and obliging, and every article is sold strictly on its merits. Two floors are occupied, their dimensions being 25 x 60 feet, and among the leading goods handled may be mentioned Fine Millinery (of which a magnificent stock is carried), Fancy Goods, Small Wares, Yarns, Underwear, Corsets, Gloves, Hosiery, Cloaks, Jackets, Wraps, Children's and Infants' Clothing, Furs, etc. A specialty is made of Paris Trimmed Pattern Hats and Bonnets, and the very latest fashionable novelties in this line are always to be found here.

Randolph, Bentley & Co.

Randolph, Bentley & Co. Builders and Dealers in Lumber, and Builders' Materials, 57 Main Street, Westerly, R. I.—There is so direct a connection between the ability and enterprise shown by those dealing in Lumber, etc., and the cost of building, that the public in general are deeply interested in the facilities enjoyed by those engaged in this important line of business, and therefore a few words concerning a leading house of this kind—that of Randolph, Bentley & Co.,—cannot fail to prove acceptable, especially as the concern in question is known to enjoy such favorable relations with producers and others as to be prepared to quote positively the lowest market rates on all the commodities handled, and to be able to fill the very heaviest orders at short notice. Spacious premises are occupied at No. 57 Main Street, and a very extensive stock of Lumber and Builders' Materials is constantly carried, while the employment of 40 men and maintenance of one of the most complete stocks of long and short Lumber and Building Materials, Wood-working plants in this section assure the prompt and accurate carrying out of all custom work. The firm do both a wholesale and retail business, and every order, large or small, is given prompt and careful attention. The original firm-name has been retained, although Mr. Randolph is dead, and the existing partners are Messrs. B. C. Bentley, C. C. Maxson and A. N. Crandall. The latter gentleman was born in the state of New York, while both his associates are natives of Westerly. Mr. Bentley is President of the Town Council, and is prominently identified with the management of the Washington Bank, and Messrs. Maxson and Crandall are also well known, aside from their connection with the enterprise to which this article has reference, Mr. Maxson being a son of the late Chas. Maxson, who was the senior member of the original firm of C. Maxson & Co., who established the lumber business in Westerly in 1843.

C. B. Cottrell & Sons

C. B. Cottrell & Sons, Printing Press Manufacturers, Westerly.—The perfection of printing apparatus is going on all the time, and although to the ordinary observer the presses of ten or a dozen years ago seemed as efficient as anything devoid of human intelligence could be, great progress has been made since then, and results attained which give an establishment equipped with the latest improved machinery an overpowering advantage over one fitted up in the style of but comparatively few years ago. Practical printers know this, and also know that "cheap" presses are too expensive to use, the result of this knowledge being an incessant and growing demand for the machinery manufactured by Messrs. C. B. Cottrell & Sons, for this firm is conceded to produce printing apparatus that is unsurpassed in the market, not only as regards efficiency and strength of design, but excellence of material and workmanship also. The business was founded by Messrs. Cottrell & Babcock in 1855, and the present firm was formed in 1880. It consists of Mr. C. B. Cottrell, a native of Westerly; Mr. E. H. Cottrell, born in the same town; and Messrs. Chas. P. Cottrell and C. B. Cottrell, Jr., who were born in Stonington, Ct. The concern have an office at No. 8 Spruce St., New York, and a Western office at No. 292 Dearborn St., Chicago, their factory in Westerly being one of the largest establishments of the kind in the country, as it has need of being, for the product is sold throughout the civilized world, and very extensive facilities are absolutely necessary to supply the steadily growing demand. The premises utilized cover an area of 7 acres, and employment is given to 300 men. The firm hold more than 75 patents on their productions, the most important being those relating to their air spring, which is admitted to be far ahead of anything else of the kind ever placed on the market. A magnificently gotten-up illustrated catalogue is issued by this representative house, and printers will find the time spent in examining it very profitably invested.

Mechanics Savings Bank

Mechanics Savings Bank, of Westerly. —A man who makes a practice of spending less than he earns, may or may not be on the "road to wealth," but one thing at least is sure —he is bound to secure himself and family against privation or want so far as his ability and circumstances will allow. Such a man can face sickness or "hard times" with a clear conscience at all events, for he did what he could in time of comparative prosperity, and hence has no regrets to hamper him when adversity is to be overcome. Some people never learn that there is happiness in saving money as well as in spending it, and therefore are very apt to pity the saving man who denies himself things he can do without for the sake of putting more money in the bank, but their pity is not wanted, for the simple reason that such a man is happier and more contented than those who never get ahead in the world, and who will realize some day that sickness or age has overtaken them and their families and found them destitute. Saving habits are to be encouraged even more for the good of the community than that of individuals, and the encouragement given by the Mechanics Savings Bank is of a kind that tells forcibly and continuously, for this institution provides a secure place for deposits, pays a liberal rate of interest and transacts business with depositors with a most commendable and gratifying absence of "red tape," and useless formalities of all kinds. It was incorporated in 1870, and the $800,000 now held on deposit attests the public confidence in the management, while the financial condition of the institution shows that confidence to be well merited. The following representative citizens act as Officers of the bank: President, W. A. Burdick; Treasurer, J. B. Foster; Trustees, W. A. Burdick, J. B. Foster, John Loveland, A. N. Lewis, I. B. Crandall, William Hoxsey, Alexander Carmichael, Orville Stillman.

Maxson & Co., (successors to C. Maxson & Co., established 1843.) Builders and Lumber Dealers. Steam Planing Mills, Doors, Sash, Blinds, Tanks, Dye Tubs, Turning, Carving, Pattern Making, Band and Jig Sawing, Brick, Lime, Cement, Drain Tile, &c., Broad street, Westerly, R. I.—The planing mills carried on by Messrs. Maxson & Co., on Broad street, ranks with the largest and best-equipped establishments of the kind in the state, the premises utilized comprising three stories of the dimensions of 50x80 feet, and being fitted up with an elaborate plant of the latest improved machinery, run by steam power. The firm do a very extensive wholesale and retail business, dealing in lumber, doors, sash and blinds, house finish, building materials, etc., including brick, lime, cement and drain tile. Order work is given prompt and careful attention, the exceptional facilities at hand enabling turning, carving, pattern making, band and jig sawing, etc., to be done at very short notice and at the lowest market rates. Employment is given to 60 assistants, and no pains are spared to maintain the unsurpassed reputation for promptness and accuracy which has so long been held. This business was founded in 1843, by Messrs. C. Maxson & Co., and has gained its present magnitude by a steady and sure process of development which is still constantly going on. The proprietors are Messrs. Jonathan and J. Irving Maxson, both of whom are so generally known throughout this section as to render extended personal mention unnecessary. They give close attention to the supervision of affairs, and are constantly striving to improve the service offered, the plant being kept up to the highest standard of efficiency and large and small orders being given equally careful attention.

H. R. Segar, (Successor to T. W. Segar,) Dealer in Coal, Wood, Hay and Fertilizers. Office, 20 Broad street. Yard, Rear 119 Main street, Westerly, R. I.—It is over thirty years since the enterprise now carried on by Mr. H. R. Segar was inaugurated. It was founded by Mr. T. W. Segar in 1853. Who was succeeded by the present proprietor in 1886, and although thirty-six years is not such a very long time in the business life of a community, still it must be confessed that decided changes have occurred in more things than one during that time. But so far as the consumption of coal is concerned a steady and rapid increase has been noticeable, and the demand for this commodity in the future, is one of the very few things that can be be predicted with any certainty. It is probable that no such serious interruption to the coal supply will ever occur again as was experienced within the two past years, but however this may be Mr. H. R. Segar may be depended upon to serve the public to the best of his ability, and to stand ready at all times to supply coal of standard quality at the lowest market rates. This house is one of the most prominent in Westerly identified with the coal trade, and has unsurpassed advantages in dealing in coal, wood, hay and fertilizers of all kinds. The premises occupied comprise an

office located at No. 20 Broad street, and a yard and store house, rear of 119 Main street, and facilities are at hand for the storing of a very large stock. An extensive retail business is done, over 3,000 tons being sold yearly. Employment is given to a sufficient force of assistants, and orders are filled with unusual accuracy and despatch.

Drs. Lewis & Spicer, Dentists, 4 Main Street, Westerly, R. I.—Give a carpenter a saw with half the teeth gone, a chisel without a cutting edge, and a plane with the iron chipped and dull, and tell him you expect him to do perfect work with such tools, and he would think you were either drunk or crazy; but very probably the same man might have a set of teeth in even worse condition than the tools you gave him, and still go on using them day after day without making any effort to have them put in order, and be wondering all the time why he was troubled with indigestion, or was not in perfect health otherwise. The function of the teeth is to prepare the food for the stomach, and defective teeth result in poorly-prepared food, especially when the process of mastication is carried on with the speed so common in these days of "rush." There is all the less excuse for being content to use injured teeth from the fact that modern dentistry stands ready to repair all such injuries in a permanent manner and at comparatively small expense. Slightly affected teeth can be filled, badly impaired ones can be extracted, and perfectly efficient artificial teeth can be substituted, and we may say right here that the pain and inconvenience popularly supposed to attend all such operations are greatly exaggerated. Much depends upon the skill of the operator and upon the perfection of the facilities at his command, but those residing in Westerly and vicinity have it in their power to avoid all uncertainty on this score, for Drs. Lewis & Spicer, whose rooms are located at No. 4 Main St., are conceded to be as expert and careful dentists as can be found in the state, and that they do not lack experience is proved by their record in Westerly alone. Dr. A. N. Lewis having begun operations here in 1861 and Dr. A. H. Spicer having become associated with him in 1864. The former is a native of New York state, and has served on the school board and as engineer of the fire department, and is now one of the trustees of the Mechanics Savings Bank. Dr. Spicer was born in Hopkinton, R. I. and is connected with the Town Council. These gentlemen are prepared to undertake Dentistry in all its branches, and their rooms are equipped with the most improved facilities. Both Gas and Ether are administered, and the most difficult operations are carried out with the speed and accuracy born of long experience. The "Sheffield Crowning Process" is employed for adjusting Gold or Porcelain Crowns to badly decayed teeth or roots; and where advisable, the use of a plate is avoided by employing "Bridge Work". Drs. Lewis and Spicer combine gentleness and thoroughness in their work, and the charges made are uniformly moderate.

EWEN & CO.
C. EWEN Gen. Manager — J. C. ARCHIE Treas.
J. MURRAY Pres.
Manufacturers of
MONUMENTAL WORK
in RED, WHITE and BLUE
WESTERLY GRANITE
FROM OUR OWN QUARRIES
FINE LETTERING AND CARVING A SPECIALTY
ALL WORK EXECUTED IN A FIRST CLASS MANNER
OUR OWN WORK
HENDEY
OFFICE & WORKS ❖ WESTERLY · R · I ·

There is a constant and increasing demand for monumental work of high character at a reasonable price, and as the concerns devoted to this line of business are not so widely known among the general public as are those carrying on most other branches of industry, we feel that we will be doing many of our readers a service when we call their attention to the facilities offered by Messrs. Ewen & Co., for this concern do cemetery work of all kinds, and are prepared to attain results and quote prices that are sure to prove entirely satisfactory. They show many beautiful and appropriate designs for monuments, headstones, tablets, etc., and those who wish to select anything in this line will find it for their interest to give Messrs. Ewen & Co. a call, as every assistance will be cheerfully rendered, and the results of long experience in the business placed at the disposal of the inquirer. The workmanship of this firm's productions is strictly first class, and the facilities are such that all orders can be filled at short notice, while, as before stated, the prices are invariably as low as the lowest.

T. H. Clark, Dealer in Fresh, Salt and Pickled Fish, Oysters, Clams, etc.: 55 Main St., Westerly.—It is universally conceded that fish make as healthful and nutritious an article of food as is to be found in the market, but it is also an accepted fact that the healthfulness and palatableness of fish are largely dependent upon its freshness and the manner in which it is handled, so it is well to use some discrimination in the placing of orders for this product, and in this connection it is natural to call attention to the advantages to be gained by dealing with Mr. T. H. Clark, located at No. 55 Main street, for since this gentleman began operations in 1888, he has gained a high reputation for furnishing uniformly first-class goods at the lowest market rates. Mr. Clark is a native of North Stonington, Ct. The premises utilized have an area of 1000 square feet, and an extensive stock is always carried, comprising fresh, salt and pickled fish, oysters, clams, etc. Mr. Clark quotes the lowest market rates on all the goods he deals in, sparing no pains to fully satisfy every customer.

J. A. Burdick, Manufacturer of Custom Shirts and Trousers of All Kinds; A Specialty of Tennis, Base-Ball and Bicycle Shirts; 28 High street, up stairs, Westerly, R. I.—No doubt ready-made shirts are "good enough" for many people who give that as the reason why they don't have their shirts made to order, but there is little sense in being content with something "good enough" when a superior article can be had at no greater expense. Yes, we know that custom-made shirts cost more than those bought ready-made, but first cost does not tell the whole story, by any means, and many a manhas found by experience that the superior durability of custom shirts makes up for the difference in price, while the superior comfort gained by their use is so much clear gain. Something depends, of course, upon with whom you place your order, but no mistake will be made if a call is made upon Mr. J. A. Burdick, for this gentleman is in a position to easily meet all honorable competition in the price and quality of his work, and to satisfy the most fastidious customers. He makes a specialty of flannel shirts to order, and carries a fine line of fancy flannels to select from. Those who have worn flannel shirts need not be told of the ease and comfort they give one in warm weather. He makes pantaloons to order as well as shirts, and attains equally excellent results in both departments of his business, while all orders can be filled at short notice.

Blake & Maxson, Dealers in Stationery, School Material, Albums, Pictures, Birthday and Holiday Cards, Notions, Etc. Pianos, Organs, and Musical Goods of all kinds. Sole agents for Mason & Hamlin, Woodard & Brown, Hallett & Cumston and New England Pianos. Mason & Hamlin, A. B. Chase, New England, and Clough & Warren Organs, Westerly, R. I.—The firm of Blake & Maxson has been well and favorably known for nearly a score of years, operations having begun in 1870. Mr. W. E. Maxson has been sole proprietor for some time but the original firm name is still adhered to. He was born in the state of New York and served two years in the army during the Rebellion. The firm occupy spacious premises on East Broad street, comprising one floor and a basement of the dimensions of 25x70 feet, together with a well-equipped shop in which the manufacture of picture-frames is carried on, the facilities being such that frames of any kind can be made to order at short notice and at very reasonable rates. A carefully chosen stock of stationery, school supplies, albums, pictures, birthday and holiday cards, notions, etc., is always on hand, and the prices quoted are uniformly low, making this a favorite resort with those wishing anything in the lines mentioned. Pianos, organs and musical merchandise of every description are also largely dealt in, the firm being sole agents for the Mason & Hamlin, Woodard & Brown, Hallett & Cumston and New England pianos, and for the Mason & Hamlin, A. B. Chase, New England and Clough & Warren organs. These instruments have too widely known a reputation to require eulogy at our hands, and we will simply say that they can be bought here at as low rates as can be quoted anywhere. Mr. Maxson gives personal attention to the tuning of pianos, and we can guarantee entire satisfaction to all who may avail themselves of his services.

I. B. Crandall & Co., Dealers in Ready-Made Clothing, Hats, Caps and Gents' Furnishings, 10 High Street, Westerly, R. I.—It is safe to assume that all of our readers are interested in the " clothing question," for everybody likes to present an attractive appearance, and on clothing must the chief dependence be placed in trying to accomplish such a result. The cost of clothing has been gradually diminishing for some years, and one only needs to visit such an establishment as that carried on by Messrs. I. B. Crandall & Co., on High st., to find convincing proof of the fact that fashionably-cut, thoroughly-made and accurately-fitting garments can now be bought for very little money. The proof will be found here if anywhere, for this firm carry an extensive and skilfully chosen stock, and are known to quote bottom prices on all the goods they handle. Mr. I. B. Crandall is a native of Genessee, N. Y., and is widely known in Westerly and vicinity, having formerly been a member of the town council, and now holding the position of representative. He has been identified with his present business since 1872, and the extent of the trade built up is the best possible evidence that the purchasing public endorse the methods which characterize its management. The store has an area of 1800 square feet, affording ample room for the accommodation of a full assortment of hats and caps, gents' furnishings, etc., as well as for the carrying of complete lines of clothing. There are 3 competent and courteous assistants employed, and the service is prompt and obliging at all times.

J. W. Vincont, Feed and Livery Stable off Main St., near Holdridge's Carriage Shop, Westerly, R. I.—The increase in the population and constant growth of any locality must have its legitimate effect upon the general business interests, and in connection with a comprehensive display of the business institutions of Westerly, it affords us no little pleasure to notice the establishment of Mr. J. W. Vincent, located on Vincent Street. This popular stable is eligible to all parts of the town, and has accommodation for a large number of horses and carriages, making it a most desirable stable for those who have horses to feed, or who wish to hire teams. Horses left to the care of this stable have every attention paid to their condition and health, and receive the best feed. Experienced assistants are employed in the various departments, and perfect satisfaction is guaranteed to all who patronize this establishment. Mr. Vincent is an experienced horseman in every respect, and thoroughly understands the proper care of stock. His prices are very reasonable, and our readers will find his establishment first-class in every respect. Though a business man in the fullest sense of the term, his genial disposition has made his Feed and Livery stable popular throughout Westerly and vicinity.

S. J. Reuter, Florist, Cut Flowers and Floral Designs, Weddings, Parties and Funerals a specialty. A large Assortment of Pot Plants always on hand. Beach St., Westerly, R. I.—There is a much more general use made of flowers in society now than was the case a few years ago, and indeed some new forms of their usefulness is constantly being made. Joy, sorrow, congratulation or condolence can all be so delicately yet adequately expressed by the employment of the proper floral emblem which often may be utilized on occasions when circumstances forbid any other gift. One of the best known gentlemen in the business in this section is the one whose card we print at the top of this notice. His greenhouses are very extensive and the grounds cover several acres. Orders can be filled without delay owing to the extensive variety of each kind at hand to select from, and mail or telegraph orders will receive prompt attention. A feature of the business which is rapidly increasing is that of landscape gardening, a specialty being made of laying out gardens and cottage lots. Many of those at Watch Hill were done by him. A number of assistants are employed and customers will be served promptly and courteously.

HISTORICAL SKETCH

OF

STONICNGTON.

As one studies some old and characteristic New England town he hardly
knows whether to wonder most at the intrepidity which induced the first settlers
to plant themselves amid so many harsh and opposing conditions or the unflinching perseverance with which they and their descendants have since gone forward
beautifying and developing every possible advantage and opening until they have
indeed cultured and multiplied the original small heritage a hundred and a thous-
and fold. Stonington, Connecticut, in its history and present prosperous state,
presents the common manifestations of such courage and triumph. In its early
history none of the first settlements had greater difficulties to overcome, and few
there are who can show such a utilization of every means of improvement and
advance.

The early history of Stonington was marked by many vicissitudes and ter-
ritorial disputes, lying as it did near the border line of three colonies. The Indian name of the present town was Pawcatuck. The earliest historical
mention is that of 1637, when in June of that year, Captain Mason on his celebrated Pequot expedition stopped one night here. On account of assistance
rendered by her to Connecticut in this expedition, Massachusetts claimed the surrounding region, including Stonington, as her reward. This did not suit Connecticut
and caused a series of disputes and counter claims. In 1643, this region was
included in a grant made to Massachusetts by the Earl of Warwick and the
Council for British America. In 1646 the little company led by John Winthrop
made their settlement near here and claimed Stonington, or Southerton as it was
then known as part of their colonial land. It was granted to them in their charter
of 1647 from the Royal Commissioners, but soon after this was revoked and the
place again assigned to Massachusetts. About this time, 1649, the first actual
settlement was made on the ground by William Cheeseborough, who had been
born in Boston, England, in 1594 and had came over with Governor Winthrop's
company. The first man to join Mr. Cheeseborough, was Thomas Stanton, the

famous Indian "Interpreter" who came here in 1650. Stanton was known throughout the colonies as the Englishman by far the best acquainted with the Indian dialects. He was given the office of Interpreter by the Connecticut Assembly in 1638, and the commissioners of the United Colonies appointed him Interpreter general. He died here in 1676. Others came in the following years, and by 1658 quite a considerable settlement had been made. In that year the people applying, received a charter from Massachusetts and the name Southerton, the place being appended to Suffolk County Massachusetts. In 1662 the Royal Commissioners decided that Southerton was in Connecticut, when they gave the colony its Royal Charter; then ensued a series of quarrels with Rhode Island, resulting in leaving Southerton in its present "statu quo." During this dubi-

WATER STREET IN 1889.

ous period, it is no wonder that the people of Stonington made a voluntary contract to sustain themselves outside of any state relations, as it practically resulted that out of the quarrel of the several states for her, Stonington was becoming deserted by them all. But at length accepting its allegiance to Connecticut, its name was changed in 1665 by the Connecticut General Assembly to Mystic, and later in the same year to present Stonington.

During the last quarter of the 17th century, Stonington was represented in the great King Philip's War by Captain George Denison, who led the Connecticut troops in the celebrated Narragansett Swamp Fight in 1775 and rendered other important services. In March 1676, with a company of volunteers, he made an invasion into the Narragansett country, and captured Canonchet, chief sachem of the tribe. When offered the option of losing life or living thereafter in peace, the iron-souled Indian replied that he "chose to die before his heart grew soft." During this same expedition, Capt. Denison's band slew and captured of the Indians, two hundred and thirty braves. Capt. Denison also represented for many years Stonington at the General Court in Hartford where he died in 1694. Another distinguished settler of the 17th century was Captain Thomas Miner, who came to Stonington, representing it in many public positions and also extending its fame by gallant service during King Philip's War.

The early part of the eighteenth century was marked by steady growth, but no distinctive features, and Stonington did not again become prominent until the outbreak of the Revolutionary War. In 1775 a British cruiser in the Sound made a spirited attack on Stonington which suffered much throughout the war from hostile marauding expeditions. A constant coast guard had to be maintained, and much of Stonington's zeal and efforts during the great struggle went out through this channel. The well known ingenuity and the warlike spirit of its citizens made them the especial object of attention and annoyance from the British armies. In 1777 they suffered another attack for the laying of torpedoes of which they were not guilty. The close of the war in 1783 was hailed with rejoicing not only because the cause in which they were so deeply interested had triumphed, but also because an opportunity was afforded them to expand and develop those sea worthy tendencies of which they had long been conscious. The close of the eighteenth and the first years of the nineteenth century witnessed quite a considerable shipping interest here. The coasting and West Indies trade made great progress in a few years, but the night-dream of prosperous voyages was soon abruptly clipped by the Embargo Act in 1807 and the other naval measures of the Government leading up to the war of 1812. In the latter, Stonington took a spirited and noteworthy part. In addition to participation in other important engagements, the year 1814 was marked at Stonington by one of the most decided repulses of the British during the war. On the 9th of August, that year, the people of Stonington were suddenly surprised by the appearance in the harbor of three British Cruisers, the Rumulus, Pactolus, and Destiny, under the command of Sir Thomas Hardy. They were rather more surprised about an hour later when a note was brought on shore to the effect that the commander proposed to bombard the town, leaving not a building standing and but one hour was allowed for the removal of the women, sick and old. Naturally the selectmen were interested to know the occasion of such action and went out to pay a call on the commander to discover it. Considerable parleying ensued, in which it was found that the people of Stonington not being careful to refrain from opposing his Majesty's interests, the latter would be conserved by the quiet and complete removal of the town from the face of the earth, and in addition since the English consul at New London had some difficulty in obtaining his wife from among the Tory prisoners, it seemed to the tender hearted British Commander that it might be some consolation to take it out on the unoffending people of Stonington. The force of these preposterous ideas became more apparent when, soon after, the Destiny came up within easy range and began to aim for the town; not being remarkably distinguished for marksmanship, little damage was done this time. The stout hearted New Englanders, however, did not propose to be knocked about in this fashion, so a large volunteer force was assembled and kept

constantly being augmented from the surrounding regions. Two eighteen pound-
ers were brought up and when the Destiny moved up nearer and began to fire
again it was met by an opposing fusilade in which it got decidedly the worse.
The American forces largely increased during the night, and when all three British vessels moved up the harbor the next day with the apparent intention of
landing they saw so large a force assembled that they made no such attempt.
Then the Destiny coming up again opened fire ;but this time was so cut up that
it soon had to beat a hasty retreat, with battered hulk and rigging, and the pumps
working hard to keep her from sinking. In all the fighting only a very few
Americans were injured, but it was reported that seventy-five of the English
mariners had been disabled. So this atrocious attempt to make a sudden con-
clusion to Stonington's history failed utterly. After the War of 1812, the shipping interest still made some advance, but not with the old time *esprit*, as the
back bone of the interest had been cut away by foolish legislation. In 1819 there
were about thirty whalers owned here but from this time on the interest became
overshadowed, and manufacturing enterprises springing up, they have ever since
steadily increased. The population in 1810 was 3,043, and the valuation in 1817
was $45,991. Among the prominent Stoningtonites of this period were; Na-
thaniel Miner, a lawyer noted no less for his brilliant acquirements than for
unimpeachable integrity; Dr. Chas. Phelps for many years a prominent member of the Judicial Bench, and Capt. Amos Palmer who represented the town
in the Legislature many years.

The town took a deep interest in the preceding events and the vital movements
of the Civil War. It contributed generously both of men and money, and
throughout the war showed a hearty and prompt spirit of co-operation with the
plans of the great war Govenor Buckingham. Many of its best loved sons per-
ished at the front, nor has the town forgotten to tenderly consecrate their memory.

Since the war the town has taken steady strides forward in spite of discourag-
ing hard times and panics. In 1870 its population was 6,313, and in 1880 this
was increased to 7,353 and is now in the region of 8,000. In 1874, the First
Congregational church celebrated its Two Hundredth Anniversary, being one of
the oldest in the state. Among the old and original families represented were
the Stantons, Palmers, Denisons, Gallups, Cheeseboroughs, Noyes, Miners, Williams, Wheelers, Pendletons, Barrows, Parks, Fishs, Deans, Wells, Cooks,
Breeds, Richardsons, Crarys, Coles, Fannings, Searls, Baileys, Mains and
Shaws. The steady and healthy growth of Stonington has tended to make a remarkable maintenance of its old families. The position of Stonington is admir-
ably adapted for the leading seaport position it occupied early in the century.
With the Pawcatuck River on one side and the Mystic River on the other it is
perfectly fitted for the reception of the largest vessels. Its harbor which opens into
Fishers Island on the South, is one of the best protected and finest along the
coast. In addition to its natural advantages, a large breakwater has been erected. Its water-power privileges connected with the Mystic and Pawcatuck Rivers,
the Copp, Stony and Anguilla brooks, are also good. The town itself contains
several villages all of which are prosperous. It contains about six square miles
or 3,840 acres. The soil is a gravelly loam, rich and finely adapted for grazing

farms, the dairy interest indeed indeed having passed all others in agricultural
importance. While the manufacturing interests of the town have been prospering, it has not forgotten more etherial but not less important interests. Educational matters have received earnest and constant attention; there are now
several finely graded schools and also one high standard high school and academy.
There are six churches belonging to the leading denominations, and the journal-
istic interests are maintained by the bright and enterprising sheet, "The Mirror."
Along with the other towns in this enviably delightful locality, Stonington has

MAIN STREET IN 1889.

been receiving of recent years increasing volumes of summer trade from visitors
who come to share its breezes and sea-side delights. The people of Stonington
themselves could hardly take a vacation to any more delightful region than their
own and many of them are able to unite the full enjoyment of sea-side life with
the expanding commercial opportunity which increases with the celebrity of the
region. As the spirit of indomitable enterprise which inspired their fathers
still lives in the sons, and the great natural advantages of Stonington are becoming more widely known, the future prosperity of the town seems safely to be
anticipated.

LEADING BUSINESS MEN OF STONINGTON.

The Boston Store, Stonington, Conn., H. H. Davis. Proprietor. Dealer in Gents' Furnishings. Dry and Fancy Goods, Boots, Shoes and Rubbers. Potter Block. Water St. The enterprise carried on under the name of The Boston Store was inaugurated by Messrs. Davidson & Rich, who were succeeded by Mr. F. E. Rich; the present proprietor, Mr. H. H. Davis having assumed control in 1882. He is a native of Stonington and has a very large circle of friends in this vicinity for he considers the interests of customers to be identical with his own and therefore has no difficulty in maintaining the most friendly relations with his patrons. The store is located at No. 150 Water street and contains a large stock of Dry and Fancy Goods, Boots, Shoes and Rubbers, also Gents' Furnishings, which is made up of fresh and seasonable articles and is always complete in every department. The store covers an area of 20 x 70 ft., so there is ample opportunity to display the goods to excellent advantage and thus make the task of selection comparatively easy. It would be useless to attempt to describe the stock in detail within the narrow limits of our available space, so we will simply say that it is constituted exclusively of fresh and desirable articles, for Mr. Davis has no time to bother with unsaleable goods and only handles such as are fashionable and popular. The latest novelties are constantly being received, and the prices quoted are low enough to explain why "carrying over" does not have to be practiced here. The assortment of Boots and Shoes comprises articles adapted to Ladies', Gentlemen's and Children's wear; no better place exists at which to get first-class Dry and Fancy Goods, Gents' Furnishings, and Boots and Shoes of all kinds.

James N. Hancox, Wholesale Dealer in Anthracite and Bituminous Coal, Kerosene, Duck and Cordage, Water Street, Stonington, Conn.—Next to food and clothing in point of importance comes fuel, and the experiences of the last year or so have served to emphasize the indispensable position held by this commodity, more strongly than ever. Coal is, of course, the main dependence of the country in the line of fuel, and although thousands of cords of wood are used annually for the same purpose, still the consumption of coal is rapidly and steadily increasing. Among the various houses located in this section which make a specialty of the handling of all kinds of coal, particular mention should be made of that of Mr. J. N. Hancox, doing business on Water street, Stonington. The enterprise carried on by Mr. Hancox is devoted to the wholesale trade. The plant utilized and located at the above named address is spacious and has ample facilities for the carrying of a heavy retail stock. Anthracite and bituminous coal are dealt in, a specialty of cargo lots is made, also kerosene, duck and cordage, and special attention is given to the prompt and accurate delivery of orders, the lowest market rates being always adhered to, and equal advantages are offered to customers in all departments of the business. Located at the terminus of the N. Y. P. & B. R. R., and being the sole shippers at this point, they have unequalled facilities for supplying their many large customers. They supply the factories, mills and villages on this line and its branches. Prompt shipment and low prices are guaranteed. The office being connected with all points by telephone.

James Pendleton, No. 2 Potter Block, Stonington, Conn., dealer in Fancy and Family Groceries, Beef, Mutton, Veal, Poultry, Game, etc., Vegetables of all kinds in their season. Particular attention paid to private families. Goods delivered to any part of the city free of charge.—Much or little can be meant by the term "Fancy Groceries" according to the way in which it is used, but in its legitimate sense, it includes an immense variety of commodities, for new articles have been added to the list, until now it has reached formidable proportions. Probably as fine a stock of fancy and family groceries as is to be found is this vicinity, is that carried by Mr. James Pendleton, at his establishment at No. 2 Potter Block, for Mr. Pendleton makes a specialty of such goods and handles them very extensively. His premises comprise a store 20 by 64 feet in size and a store-room. Employment is given to two competent and well-informed assistants. Among the articles included in the stock to which we wish to call special attention, is the line of meats offered, for this is exceptionally complete and is made up of beef, mutton, veal, poultry, game, etc. A fine selection of groceries is always at hand to choose from, and the assortment of vegetables of all kinds is made up of fresh goods that are bound to suit the most fastidious. Low prices rule and customers are promptly served, and goods are delivered to any part of the city free of charge. Mr. Pendleton is a native of Stonington. He is a member of the board of Selectmen, and also one of the Burgess of the Burough.

Charles F. Fisher, Dealer in fine Custom and Ready-made Clothing. Gents' Furnishing Goods, Hats, Caps, Trunks, Valises, etc.: 135 Water street, Stonington.—Life is too short for people to become good judges of even half of the many articles called for in civilized existence, and therefore the only practical, and certainly the most convenient way of being sure of getting one's money's worth is to patronize a reliable dealer who guarantees that every article bought of him shall prove as represented. Such a one is Mr. Charles F. Fisher, doing business at No. 135 Water street, and therefore those who wish to buy anything in the line of fine custom and ready-made clothing, gents' furnishing goods, hats, caps, trunks, valises, etc., would do well to visit his store, for not only are the goods dependable and the prices low, but the stock on hand is so large and varied that it would be difficult to name anything included among the kind of goods mentioned, not comprised in it. Mr. Fisher is a native of Germany and has been identified with his business in Stonington since 1880. He gives careful personal attention to the supervision of affairs, and as employment is given to three competent and courteous assistants, callers may always depend upon receiving immediate and polite service, as well as being supplied with articles that will give entire satisfaction. The latest and most fashionable novelties in woolens are always to be found at this popular establishment, and an extensive retail trade is transacted.

Mystic Valley Water Co., office at Mystic Bridge, Stonington. Pres. Thos. E. Packer. Treas., D. B. Spalding. Sec'y, Geo. G. Grinnell.—This company was organized in 1887 with a capital of $140,000 for the purpose of introducing water into the village of Mystic Bridge, Mystic River, Noank, and Stonington Borough. The water comes from Mistuxet Brook, and has a reservoir and pumping station at Palmer's Hill, situated midway between these villages. This water will be introduced into dwellings, factories, stores, etc., at very reasonable rates and is vastly superior to well water in purity, being filtered. It is much better for washing, owing to softness, and for drinking purposes there is no danger of being contaminated by sewers, etc., etc., a common source of danger with well water. This was constructed by Messrs. Wheeler and Parks, of Boston and cost almost $150,000. It is rapidly being introduced into this section as far as mains can be laid—at present there are one hundred and seventy-five services. The pumps have a capacity of 2,000,000 gallons in 24 hours.

DR. JAMES H. WEEKS,

DENTISTRY IN ALL ITS BRANCHES.

FIRST-CLASS WORK at REASONABLE PRICES.

STONINGTON, CONN.

W. F. Broughton, dealer in all kinds of Fresh Fish, Lobsters, Oysters, Clams, Scallops, Beef, Pork, Sausage, Vegetables, &c., 65 Water Street, Stonington, Conn.—The enterprise conducted by Mr. W. F. Broughton has rapidly developed, since it was inaugurated about six years ago, he deals in fish and meats, and has built up a large trade in those commodities, and has a very large circle of friends throughout this section. Mr. Broughton now employs two assistants and his retail trade extends throughout the trade radius of Stonington. Fresh fish, lobsters, oysters, clams, scallops, beef, pork, sausage, vegetables, etc., are largely dealt in, the goods being carefully selected and all tastes being catered to, so that whether fresh or shell fish, choice cuts of meats or less costly portions be wanted, Mr. Broughton is prepared to supply the want at lowest market rates. The premises occupied are located at No. 65 Water Street, and cover an area of 18 by 35 feet. Mr. Broughton has catered to local trade long enough to become thoroughly familiar with just what the residents of this vicinity prefer, and as a consequence our readers will find his stock exceptionally desirable in every respect, all orders being accurately filled and promptly delivered.

Dr. C. E. Brayton & Co., Pharmacists;

77 Main St., corner High, Stonington, Conn.—
If every druggist were also a physician, the
convenience of the public would undoubtedly
be served; but as such is not the case, the best
thing to do is to take advantage of the opportunities offered by those who do combine these
important points. Among these, we take
pleasure in calling particular attention to the
firm of C. E. Brayton & Co., whose establishment is located at No. 77 Main street, for Dr.
Brayton and Mr. C. T. Willard, P. H. G., who
is in charge of the store, are thoroughly competent and experienced chemists, Dr. C. E.
Brayton being also a thoroughly skilled
practicing physician; and as he offers consul-
tations at all hours, the benefits of his services
are within the reach of all. The establishment
comprises the entire lower floor of the block,
and includes reception room, private office, etc.,
and a drug store 25 x 50 feet. Three reliable
and well informed clerks are employed, and
the large stock of drugs, medicines, chemicals,
toilet and fancy articles, stationery, etc., is
carefully selected from the most reliable sources, and always kept complete in every department. Prescriptions are compounded at short
notice day or night, and the charges made are
always as low as is consistent with the use of
ingredients of the best quality, and customers
are at all times assured of prompt and courteous
attention.

August Muller, Manufacturer to order and
Dealer in Furniture, Mattresses, Window
Shades and Fixtures, Curtains, Cornices, Picture Frames, etc.; Coffins and Caskets of the
most approved make; Particular attention paid
to Embalming; Corner Gold and Pearl streets,
Stonington.—The establishment conducted by
Mr. August Müller is widely known as the
head-quarters for furniture, bedding, window
shades, etc., for the proprietor has carried on
operations in Stonington for nearly 35 years,
having begun business here in 1855. He is a
native of Germany, and is one of the best known
personally of all our local merchants. The
premises made use of comprise 3 floors of the
dimensions of 55 x 68 feet, and are located at
the corner of Gold and Pearl Sts. A very extensive stock is carried, and every facility is at
hand for the making to order of window shades,
curtains, picture frames, mattresses, etc.
The stock on hand comprises the latest novelties in such goods, as well as full lines of
staple styles, and we need hardly say that Mr.
Müller's long experience in the business, and
the magnitude of his trade, enable him to
quote positively bottom prices on all the goods
handled. Employment is afforded to 3 efficient
assistants, and every caller may depend upon
receiving immediate and courteous attention.
A large assortment of coffins and caskets of all
approved makes is constantly on hand, and
funeral undertaking is attended to at very short
notice. Particular attention is given to embalming, and every necessary facility is at
hand to carry on operations to the best possible advantage.

Moses Pendleton, Dealer in Groceries and
Provisions, Wholesale and Retail Dealer in
Coal, 66 Water Street, Brick Store. Agency for
Staten Island Dye Works, Stonington, Conn.
It would be difficult if not impossible to find
a more carefully selected stock of Groceries and
Provisions etc., than that carried by Mr. Moses
Pendleton doing business on Water street, for
this popular gentleman has built up his present
extensive retail trade by furnishing the public
with superior goods, and appreciates the patronage bestowed upon him far too highly to risk the
loss or diminution of it by offering commodities
that cannot be guaranteed to give satisfaction.
The business was started by its present proprietor in 1846 and he is thus widely known in
Stonington and vicinity. The premises made
use of are equipped with all necessary facilities
for the proper storage and handling of the heavy
stock carried. The prices quoted are as low as
can be named on goods of equal excellence,
and customers are at all times assured prompt
and courteous attention. Groceries, Provisions
and Coal are very extensively handled and all
orders received for the same are promptly, accurately and conscientiously filled. In the
rear of the store is Pendleton's Long Wharf
which is nearly 500 feet in length and has a
pipe extending the entire distance for supplying vessels, steamers, yachts, etc., with water.
It affords ample wharfage for shipping.

C. H. Crandall. Sails, Awnings and all
kinds of Canvass Work, Water Street, Stonington, Conn.—The expression "white-wings," as
used to indicate the sails of a vessel, looks and
sounds very poetical, no doubt, but those in a
position to realize how much hard and faithful
work is called for in the fitting and making of
these same "white-wings" know that there is
much more truth than poetry connected with
them. Only by varied and long continued experience can the trade of the sail-maker be
mastered, and very few of those engaged in
this industry can equal the record of Mr. Crandall. The general introduction of large plate-
glass show windows has created an active and
ever-growing demand for awnings, for goods
exposed behind these great sheets of glass are
soon faded out of all resemblance to their original condition if the sun is allowed to beat upon
them, no little skill is required in order to
make awnings that will look well, wear well
and work well and it is universally conceded
that Mr. C. H. Crandall turns out work of this
kind that will compare favorably with any in
the market. The awnings on the "Watch Hill"
were made by Mr. Crandall. awnings for yachts
a specialty. So far as experience is concerned,
he is certainly well-qualified to win success in
this line of business, for he has been identified
with it ever since 1865, having at that time
succeeded Mr. J. Blackledge. Mr. Crandall
was born in Stonington and is very widely
known here, having formerly been a member
of the Board of Selectmen. His establishment
is located on Water Street, and is of the dimensions of 25x50 feet, being fitted up with all
necessary facilities, not only for awning making, but also for sail making and in fact every

description of canvass work. Employment is given to 3 experienced and careful assistants, and orders can be filled at very short notice, moderate charges being made and no defective work being knowingly allowed to leave the shop.

Vincent's Restaurant and Café

Vincent's Restaurant and Café, Meals at all hours, Branch Watch Hill, opp. Post-office. Tifts' Block, Stonington, Conn.—Mr. L. H. Vincent began business in Stonington in 1886, and if the enterprise with which he is identified has already become one of the most popular in town it is because he has striven to learn the wants of the public and has spared neither trouble, or expense, in satisfying them. He was born in Providence, R. I., and is probably one of the best known men in Stonington, for the nature of his business favors the making of acquaintances, and after eating one of his finely cooked dinners you feel as though he were a personal friend of yours. The premises occupied are located in Tifts Block and are of the dimensions of 20x60 feet, and have a seating capacity for forty guests, and a first-class Restaurant and Café is carried on. Mr. Vincent is prepared to cater for parties, balls etc., and meals may be obtained here at all hours, and served at very liberal rates. Mr. Vincent supplies his tables with choice food and plenty of it, and those who go hungry from his establishment (if anybody ever does) have only themselves to thank for it, for he stints the supply of nothing, and his prices are low enough to come within the means of all. Four competent assistants are constantly employed, and good management pervades the establishment, and the service is prompt accurate and courteous at all times. Mr. Vincent's business is rapidly increasing and he well deserves the success he has won.

A. B. Miller

A. B. Miller, Iron and Brass Founder; Iron Fence, Grate Bars, Sash Weights, Machinery Castings, etc.; East Grand St., Stonington.—The iron and brass foundry of which Mr. A. B. Miller is the proprietor, is one of the best equipped establishments of the kind in this section of the state, and is also one of the best known, for it was opened more than a score of years ago, and has long held its present leading position. Mr. Miller was born in Providence, R. I., and has a very large circle of friends in Stonington and vicinity, he having at one time been a Burgess of the Borough. The premises utilized by him are located on East Grand St., and are 60 x 120 feet in dimensions, exclusive of a spacious brass shop. The manufacture of iron fence, grate bars, sash weights, machinery castings, etc., is extensively carried on; also a steam heater which is largely used in Westerly and vicinity, iron and brass founding to order being made a specialty, and being assured immediate, painstaking and satisfactory attention. Employment is given to from 5 to 12 assistants, and Mr. Miller gives the business careful personal supervision, thus assuring a continuance of the highly satisfactory service which has so long been afforded, and which has given the enterprise its present representative position.

C. S. Ryon

C. S. Ryon, Livery, Sale and Boarding Stable, Elm Street, Stonington, Conn.—Considering that it is almost impossible to find two men who will agree on all points as to what constitutes a good horse, it is not at all strange that no Livery Stable keeper has ever lived who perfectly satisfied *everybody*, but of course there is a good deal of difference observable in the methods practiced at the various public stables, and as we wish our readers to go where they will be assured prompt and polite attention, and thoroughly first-class service in every respect, we take pleasure in calling their favorable attention to the establishment conducted by Mr. C. S. Ryon, on Elm Street, for this is one of the best-equipped Livery, Sale and Boarding Stables in Stonington and vicinity, and the management is liberal, enterprising and reliable. Mr. Ryon is a native of Mystic, Conn., and founded the business in question in 1882. He gives careful personal attention to the filling of orders and sees that the instructions of patrons are faithfully carried out. Some excellent teams are available for Livery purposes, and the charges made are uniformly moderate. Horses will be taken to board and assured the best of care, and an abundance of proper food, employment being given to two assistants and the premises being kept in first-class condition. Orders for Trucking are also promptly and satisfactorily filled, moderate prices being quoted in every instance. Mr. Ryon goes West every spring and purchases large numbers of fine horses which he offers at reasonable rates.

H. C. Stanton

H. C. Stanton, dealer in Foreign and Domestic Fruits, Confectionery, Cigars and Tobacco, Billiard and Pool Rooms, also Livery Stable, 143 Water Street, Stonington, Conn.—There are so many things to mention concerning the business carried on by Mr. H. C. Stanton, that we scarcely know where to begin, for this gentleman is an extensive dealer in foreign and domestic fruits, confectionery, cigars, Tobacco, etc. and also has a billiard and pool room, and conducts a well-equipped livery stable. He began operations about thirty-five years ago, and is almost universally known in this vicinity. Mr. Stanton is a native of Stonington, and gives careful personal attention to the many details of his business and spares no pains to offer just such goods as the public want and to quote bottom prices at all times. His business is much too large to admit of our describing it in detail, but we have already mentioned the principal articles dealt in and will only add that they are guaranteed to prove as represented in every instance, and cannot fail to satisfy the most critical. Employment is given to efficient assistants and prompt and polite attention is assured to all. Mr. Stanton is prepared to furnish first-class teams, at short notice, and makes his prices within the reach of all. The result being that he is well patronized by the public, who are quick to take advantage of such liberal offers, and not at all backward in showing their appreciation of the same.

H. E Conant, Silk Manufacturer. Stonington.—Although the manufacture of silk has long been one of the greatest industries of the country, it may be said to be as yet but in its infancy, for all signs point to a development of which at the present time we can have but a vague idea. Chief among these signs must be placed the prosperity of individual enterprises, for certainly when nearly all the different establishments devoted to a certain line of business are prosperous, the inference is plain that that business is sure to develop greatly. For instance, there is the undertaking carried on by Mr. H. E. Conant. This was formerly located in Willimantic, but was removed to Stonington, in 1886. The premises utilized are located off Water St. and are of the dimensions of 24 x 140 feet. They are equipped with the most improved machinery throughout, and employment is given to 25 assistants, the annual production being over 15,000 lbs. It is increasing all the time, and will doubtless continue to do so, for Mr. Conant's productions are equal to the best. Orders are filled at short notice, and the lowest market rates are quoted. He is a native of Mansfield, Ct., and has had extended experience in connection with his present line of business. Mr. Conant gives careful personal supervision to affairs, and spares no pains to attain the best possible results. Mr. Conant is also the inventor of a machine for spinning and winding silk. The advantage of this device is shown in the "take up" motion which not being stationary, will take up and prevent "kinks," thereby improving the quality of the goods. These he proposes to shortly introduce on the market and applications from manufacturers will be answered promptly and very favorable terms made for their introduction.

S. H. Chesebro. Dealer in Groceries and Provisions, Flour, Meal and Feed, 246 Water Street, Stonington, Conn. Mr. S. H. Chesebro has carried on business in Stonington since 1859, and has long held a leading position in the ranks of those engaged in the handling of Groceries, Provisions, Flour, Meal and Feed. Mr. Chesebro was born in Stonington and is widely and favorably known in this vicinity. The premises made use of comprise a store 20 x 70 feet and a storehouse; a very heavy stock being constantly carried, an extensive retail business is done. As Mr. Chesebro's facilities are familiar to the residents of Stonington, we will not dwell upon them, but speak especially of the advantages offered to customers. A very complete assortment of standard and popular brands of Flour is at hand to choose from, and the very lowest market rates are invariably quoted, the goods being fully guaranteed to prove as represented. Meal and Feed of all Kinds are also furnished in quantities to suit at bottom prices. Three efficient assistants are employed and every order for anything in the line of Groceries, Provisions, Flour, and Feed will be given prompt and painstaking attention. Mr. Chesebro is a native of Stonington, and is well known throughout the community, and has held the office of Selectman during the years 1872-7-and 8, and was Representative in 1874.

The Stonington Savings Bank, Stonington, Ct.. Water street.—That "example is better than precept," is an axiom, the truth of which needs no demonstration, and for this reason there is more genuine effectiveness in the lessons inculcated by one well-managed and progressive savings institution than there can be in any argument—no matter how logical or eloquent—tending to show the advantages of saving habits. The moralist and economist say: "Save what you can of your earnings, and when age, sickness, or trouble of any kind comes, you will be prepared to meet it." The savings bank don't say, but shows that your neighbor, John Smith, bought a house last week with the accumulated principal and interest of a few years, and then you, having the case put before you in so substantial a form, will think "well, Smith is no smarter than I am; there are still houses to be bought, money to be saved, and a safe bank to put it in, and I am going to take advantage of the opportunity and follow this example. and you do, you become a better citizen, a more faithful worker. It is just because savings banks work such changes that they are of incalculable advantage to any community. The Stonington Savings Bank is a notable example of what such an institution should be, and we are glad to know that a confidence is reposed in it by the public that is fully justified by the facts. The bank was incorporated in May, 1850, and its resources have steadily increased until they have reached very large proportions. The officers are as follows: President, Oliver B. Grant; vice-president, Moses Pendleton; secretary and treasurer, Daniel B. Spalding; trustees, Oliver B. Grant, Moses Pendleton, Daniel B. Spalding, Richard A. Wheeler, Lodowick N. Latham, Jos. E. Smith, Oliver D. Chesebro, Wm. E. Brewster, Wm. J. H. Pollard, Moses A. Pendleton. These gentlemen are known and esteemed throughout the community, and the bank is sure to maintain its present exceptionally high reputation as long as its affairs are in such able and experienced hands.

H. N. Wheeler, Jeweler, 123 Water Street, Stonington, Connecticut. Waltham Watches a Specialty.—Mr. H. N. Wheeler is a native of this town, and since he began operations in the Watch and Jewelry business here in 1881, he has built up a thriving trade, for he makes it a point to handle only reliable goods and to quote moderate rates on every article sold. The premises occupied are located at No. 123 Water street Mr. Wheeler carries a fine assortment of watches, Jewelry etc., including all styles of the popular "Waltham Watches" as well as others of standard make, the grades and prices being so varied that all tastes and purses can be suited. Particular attention is given to the handling of Jewelry of all kinds, some beautiful and original styles being shown and bottom prices being named on all of them. Watches are carried in stock and any make ordered if desired; those wishing a handsome and reliable time keeper would do well to look over this stock.

R. P. Babcock & Co. Livery and Boarding Stables, High Street, Stonington, Conn.— That Stonington is a remarkably pleasant place to visit is the practically unanimous verdict of those who have personally tested the matter, and not the least of the attractions which appeal to visitors are the good roads and striking scenery which make driving so enjoyable. But something more than this is necessary in order to get genuine pleasure out of driving, and that is just such accommodations as are furnished by Messrs. R. P. Babcock & Co. who carry on a first-class Livery and Boarding Stable on High Street. This establishment was founded about thirty years ago by Mr. R. P. Babcock who is a native of R. I. and conducted by him until 1888, when Messrs. J. E. Curtin and T. W. Garrity, (both natives of Stonington, Conn.) were admitted to the business. Since which date the firm-name has been as at present, R. P. Babcock & Co. These gentlemen have made their establishment one of the most popular stables in this vicinity and offer advantages to their customers that fully explain how this success has been won. Single and Double Teams may be hired at very reasonable rates, and both the horses and the vehicles will have the closest inspection. There are three assistants employed and orders can be filled at very short notice at all times. Horses taken to board are given comfortable quarters and the best of care, and as this firm make a specialty of this line of their business, those wishing to place their horses with responsible parties would do well to give Messrs. Babcock & Co. a call.

Miss M. A. Paine, first class Millinery, Ladies' Furnishing Goods, &c., Potter Block, Water Street, Stonington, Ct.—It is very evident that the establishment conducted by Miss M. A. Paine is very popular among the ladies of Stonington, for not only is it very generously patronized but any inquiries concerning it are sure to meet with a very favorable response. Miss Paine is a native of East Greenwich, and has carried on the enterprise in question since 1859. Her millinery establishment is located in Potter Block on Water Street, and has an area of 500 feet, being very completely fitted-up and containing a most attractive and tastefully arranged stock of millinery goods, and ladies' furnishings in general. Miss Paine employs two assistants in busy season and the many orders received for custom work are filled at short notice. The latest novelties in millinery goods are always to be found in her assortment, as she keeps herself thoroughly well-informed concerning the newest dictates of fashion and gives customers the full benefit of such knowledge. Moderate prices are quoted in every department of the business and goods are cheerfully shown at all times.

Jerome S. Anderson, Insurance Agency, Room 2, Grant Block, Water Street, Stonington, Conn.—In a thriving business community such as Stonington, there must of necessity be a great deal of insurable property in the way of real-estate, machinery etc., and as no live business man nowadays allows his property to remain uninsured, it follows that there is plenty for a live agent as Mr. Jerome S. Anderson to do, in the line of issuing new policies and renewing old ones. This gentleman is one of the best-known of our active business men, and has been engaged in his present line since 1872. Mr. Anderson is a native of Philadelphia, Pa. He is well known throughout Stonington and vicinity. He served in the army during the Rebellion, has been on the Board of Education for seventeen years, also Justice of the Peace, and was clerk and treasurer of the Burough. He is also editor of the Stonington Mirror and Mystic Journal. Among the Insurance Companies represented by him may be mentioned. The

Commercial Union of		England.
London Assurance	"	"
No. British Mercantile	"	"
American	"	New York.
Fidelity & Casualty	"	"
Loyds Plate Glass	"	"
Jersey City	"	New Jersey.
Granite State	"	Portsmouth, N. H.
Connecticut	"	Hartford, Conn.
Meriden	"	Meriden. "

These companies are too well and favorably known to render it necessary to call attention to the advantages derivable from holding policies in them, and we will therefore simply say that those wanting insurance that insures, can do no better than make choice of these companies. Mr. Anderson can issue policies on as favorable terms as any Agent can. Prompt and painstaking attention is given to all orders received, and the system in operation is so admirable and complete as to ensure that all the many interests confided to him will receive due consideration.

Atwood Machine Company, Manufacturers of Improved Silk Machinery; Atwood's Improved Guide System and Special Appliances; Stonington, Conn.—The improved silk machinery, made by the Atwood Machine Company, is the result of years of experience in this special line of manufacture, and is conceded to be fully equal to the best in every respect, including strength and efficiency of design, thoroughness of construction, and durability under the severest conditions of practical use. The distinguishing features of this machinery are very generally known among silk manufacturers, and that their merits are appreciated is clearly shown by the constant and growing demand for them, the Atwood Machine Company having to employ some 200 hands, and to operate one of the most extensive establishments of the kind in this country. The business was founded many years ago by Mr. J. E. Atwood, and the present company is composed of Messrs. John E. and Eugene Atwood, the latter gentleman being treasurer and manager. He is a son of the founder of the enterprise, and having "grown up" in the business" is thoroughly familiar with it in every detail. The premises in use comprise a main building, 4 stories in height and 105 x 45 feet in dimensions, with one wing measuring 31 x 86 feet, and another 38 x 77 feet in size, these wings being 3 stories high. At the west end of this structure is a brick building, 60 x 70 feet in dimensions, and utilized as a boiler and engine house, japan house, blacksmith shop, etc. There is also a large foundry, a two-story stock house, besides sand sheds, storehouses, dock, etc. Power is afforded by a 100 horse engine, and from 175 to 200 assistants are employed. The company hold many patents on their machinery, and are constantly striving to add to its efficiency in all practical ways. They are prepared to fill orders at short notice, and the exceptionally complete facilities enjoyed enable all competition to be met, both as regards cost and excellence of workmanship.

—

H. J. Kelsey & Co. Druggists, Stonington, Conn. This firm have had an extensive experience as Druggists, having been engaged in this line of business, prior to succeeding Mr. George D. Brown in 1883. Mr. Kelsey is a native of Middletown, Conn., and is well known throughout Stonington. The premises utilized comprise a store 20 x 40 feet in size, and are very conveniently fitted up. A carefully selected stock of Drugs, Medicines, and Chemicals is always on hand, and particular attention is given to the compounding of Physicians prescriptions. Messrs. Kelsey & Co. "run no chances" when engaged in this line of work and neglect no precaution to ensure absolute accuracy in every respect. They have the most improved modern facilities and are in a position to fill orders at short notice as well as at reasonable rates. Messrs. Kelsey & Co. are located at No. 63 Water street and in addition to Drugs, etc., deal in Toilet and Fancy Articles to a considerable extent and an efficient assistant is employed, so that callers may depend upon receiving prompt and courteous attention; and as no pains are spared to make the

service as perfect as possible, it most certainly deserves the success that has been won. This firm also are proprietors of a new and unrivalled remedy for constipation, LAXO which may be obtained of all druggists or sent prepaid for 25 cents.

—

R. H. Taylor, Groceries and Provisions; Grand St., Stonington.—The importance of purchasing food supplies from a dealer who may be entirely depended upon to furnish strictly reliable goods, is of course too obvious to require demonstration; and that it is generally appreciated by the residents of Stonington, needs no further proof than that afforded by the liberal patronage bestowed upon the enterprise conducted by Mr. R. H. Taylor on Grand street, for this gentleman has a well deserved reputation for handling dependable goods, and quotes such low prices as to make the increasing magnitude of his business all the more easily understood. Mr. Taylor is a native of Stonington, and has carried on business operations here for over 30 years; and is so widely known as to require no extended personal mention. He utilizes a store measuring 20 x 50 feet and containing a heavy stock of choice family groceries and provisions of all kinds. These goods are offered in quantities to suit at the lowest market rates, and as employment is given to efficient and courteous assistants, customers may safely depend upon receiving prompt and polite service.

First National Bank

OF STONINGTON.

꧁ FORMERLY OCEAN BANK ꧂

Incorporated As State Bank In 1851,

Reorganized As a National Bank

In 1865.

Capital, $200,000.

OFFICERS.

PRESIDENT,	WM. J. H. POLLARD.
VICE PRESIDENT,	O. B. GRANT.
CASHIER,	N. A. PENDLETON.

DIRECTORS.

WM. J. H. POLLARD,

O. B. GRANT,

WM. E. BREWSTER,

MOSES PENDLETON,

MOSES A. PENDLETON.

F. E. Hammond, News Depot. Books' Stationery, Magazines, Toys, Tobacco, and Cigars. A Full Line of Lovell and Seaside Libraries, 133 Water, Corner of Grand street, Stonington, Conn.—An enterprise of special interest to the people of Stonington, and one that will be of value to learn something about in this volume, is the Periodical and Stationery business, conducted by Mr. F. E. Hammond who has been identified with it since 1887, having at that date succeeded Mrs. M. J. Pendleton. His News Depot is located at No. 133 Water St. corner of Grand street, where he transacts a large retail trade in Books, Stationery, Toys, Tobacco, Cigars, etc. The business of this establishment is steadily increasing and its resources are ample to meet all demands made upon it, and its policy entitles it to the consideration of the trade, who will find assured advantage in dealing here. Mr. Hammond employs three competent assistants, and his store is under able and efficient management. A full and complete line of the Lovell and Seaside Libraries is carried. Mr. Hammond is a native of Stonington, a gentleman thoroughly conversant with the minutest details concerning his business to which he gives his close personal attention, and our citizens are sure that they can obtain here the latest and most popular publications of the day, and we can commend them to no better house in Stonington.

B. F. Ross, Restaurant, Water street, Stonington, Conn.—Among what may be called the institutions of Stonington, mention should be made of B. F. Ross's restaurant on Water street, for this establishment is known to very many people and in some respects has no equal in this vicinity. It occupies premises of the dimensions of 20 by 70 feet, and those who appreciate good food neatly served amid pleasant surroundings, will thank us after giving this restaurant a trial, for causing them to patronize it. Mr. Ross, established the enterprise in question in 1865, it being the oldest place of the kind in town. He employs experienced assistants and places his prices at such figures that everybody wonders "how he can do it." The best table board is furnished, and it shall be remembered that the food, as well as the service is first-class and that great pains are taken to satisfy every guest. Mr. Ross furnishes the best food to be found in the market, and guarantees that it shall be courteously and promptly served, and as forty guests can be comfortably seated at a time, we would advise all who are in want of a well cooked and nicely served meal to patronize this establishment. Mr Ross is also prepared to cater for parties, balls, etc., and guarantees that all orders entrusted to him shall be satisfactorily filled and executed.

James H. Brown, Wholesale and Retail Dealer in Beef, Pork Lamb, Mutton, Veal Poultry, etc., No. 121 Water Street, Stonington, Conn. The establishment carried on by Mr. James H. Brown was established in 1836 by Mr. A. Brown, the present proprietor having conducted it since 1885, Mr. James H. Brown is a native of Stonington and doubtless owes no little of the success he has gained, to the thorough practical knowledge of his business in every detail. The premises occupied are 30 by 60 feet in dimensions and are located at No. 121 Water street, and contain a very extensive stock of meats of all kinds. All classes of trade are catered to, and equal provision is made for those who want the very highest grade of goods obtainable and those who prefer the cheaper kinds. Employment is given to an efficient assistant and customers may depend upon receiving prompt and careful attention. Beef, Pork, Lamb, Mutton, Veal, Poultry etc., are handled by Mr. Brown, and the lowest market rates are quoted both on wholesale and retail orders. The meats etc. sold at this establishment have gained a high reputation among the most fastidious buyers, for the quality is simply unsurpassed, and no fancy prices are named at any time. In fact, reliable goods at bottom rates, is the motto of the proprietor, and there is no dealer better prepared to carry out this policy to its fullest extent.

HISTORICAL SKETCH

OF

MYSTIC.

Among all the charming villages and towns that are strung like a line of pearls along the northern shore of Long Island Sound, the visitor will hardly find one that will so completely and lastingly hold his fancy and memory as the village of Mystic. It is nominally a part of Stonington, but it has long had a history and life distinctively its own. It is one of the anomalies of town growth, how the name Mystic was conceived, and how it has lingered after being officially annulled. Whether the General Court which met in 1665 had some members poetically inclined who had been touched by the weirdness of the ocean scenery in this region, or whether those representing the place had memories of an English home in mind is not known, but in any case that year, what is now the whole town of Stonington, before that known as Southerton, received from the legislature the new name of Mystic. But, poetry perhaps being counterbalanced by some cold foresight of the value of its granite hills, early the next year, 1666, the name of the town was changed to Stonington. But the name that had only lasted half a year, clung still to the upper part of the town, having apparently found a pleasing lodgment in the hearts of the sea-faring people here, who had themselves so often caught glimpses of the mystery of the sea. From the first, the sea-going people, who formed so large a part of Stonington's population, seemed to cluster together here. Being at the head of navigation, just far enough and not too far away from the shore, the old sea-captains and the common sailors too, who had been far enough around the world to know a pleasant place when they saw it, soon chose this spot, planted their land-homes here and often a vision of its beauty came across them as they steered away through smooth and stormy seas. As the roof-trees sent off branches the little settlement grew into a village, and the village into a town; the number of vessels freighted with human hopes and memories which it sent out on the deep kept increasing, and it may be said to Mystic's honor, that it has clung to its early dream of sea-won conquests more tenaciously through foreign and home

THE SQUARE - MYSTIC BRIDGE.

opposition, than most of its sister sea-ports. Even yet it can count its noble names of sea-kings of the Viking stock, and it has never lost its early charm for the old sea-captains who love to gather and settle here, sailing over again with one another the old voyages and reviving the heroic memories of the past. Although but a small settlement during the revolution, Mystic at that time contributed some of her sturdiest warriors to Stonington's patriot forces but it was in the war of 1812 that she began to make prominently evident of what metal she was made. A large part of the vessels, (sailing from this port during the war) which cleared the British cruisers all along the Atlantic coast, winning many Union-Jacks and prizes, were fitted out by and with Mystic men. Especially famed was the privateer " Hero " of Mystic whose swift wings and flashing prowess many an English convoy had cause to rue, and one of whose exploits was the recapturing of the sloop " Vox " out of the hands of a Britisher who had thought to make it a prize. And when the dastardly attempt was made by Commodore Hardy to annihilate Stonington in August 1669, then the valor and patriotism of Mystic flashed out at white heat. Among the earliest who rallied to keep off the insolent foe, were Capt. Jedediah Holmes, Deane Gallup, Fred Haley, Jesse Deane, N. Cliff and Jedediah Reed of Mystic, and throughout the three gloomy days of terror her representatives were ever in the front.

The general decline of the shipping interests during the succeeding decades was of course a great barrier to Mystic's advance but she has held to her darling enterprise up to the present time and still has quite a considerable trading and ship-building business. But the great feature of the century was the introduction of railroads and the development of the manufacturing interests, which have contributed most in recent times to the material up-building of the town. During the civil war, Mystic joined heartily with the rest of the town in contributing of its men and means to the suppression of the rebellion, and since has gone steadily forward prospering and to prosper. The census of 1880 assigned to the combined villages of older Mystic, (or the Head of the River, as sometimes called), Mystic Bridge and Mystic River, all three being comprised under the name of Mystic, a total population of 2,400, and this has since increased to over 3000. The railroad station on the shore line is situated at Mystic Bridge, and is about eight miles from New London. In all three villages combined there are six churches, two national banks and a number of extensive and growing commercial enterprises, each village being the center of a thriving and prosperous community. Among the most prominent of Mystic's honored names are those of the Mallorys father and sons, far-seeing and able business men, founders of steamship lines, prudent conservative legislators. Clark Greenman and the Greenman Bros., have also gained an honored name for the skill and industry displayed in the founding of the Sabbatarian community known as Greenmanville. In all the departments of town life Mystic has shown an independent and straight-forward spirit that has made it very influential in the development along all lines. Educational and religious interests have received careful and unwearied attention, while the public work has not been neglected, the militia, fire and police departments being steadily maintained.

Bounded by gently sloping hills, with two rivers winding in and out around it, with a touch of salt in cooler air from the ocean, to which a short and pleasant row down the river will soon take one. Mystic comes as near the ideal summer home as anything could in this yet unperfected spheroid. A place for a poet to while away innumerable happy hours, for the tired city denizen to gain the most soothing and strengthening influences of nature.

LEADING BUSINESS MEN OF MYSTIC.

Groton Savings Bank, Mystic River, Conn. —The principal difference between the man who believes in "luck" and he who does not is simply this—the former is very apt to sit down and wait for success to come to him, while the latter gets up early and goes out to hunt it up. Many an article has been written, and many a sermon has been preached on the utilization of present opportunities, but the importance of such a practice is too seldom borne in mind by the thousands who have their way to make in the world. Let a young man resolve to save *something*, however small, every week that he works, and he has made a resolution which, if honestly carried out, is positively sure to be of incalculable benefit to him. A man, who can save money when earning but $6.00 a week, can surely save more when he comes to earn twice that amount, but on the other hand, experience proves, that one who can't or won't save anything from small wages, is not at all liable to do any better even when his salary is doubled. Some of our readers may be disposed to laugh at this statement, but it is susceptible of proof, and practical and unprejudiced men will admit its truth. As to the possibility of saving from a small salary, we have only to say that by far the larger portion of the immense sum held on deposit at the Groton Savings Bank is the accumulation of those who have put aside comparatively trivial amounts from time to time until the present imposing sum total has been attained. This bank was incorporated in 1854, and may justly be taken as an example, as it is one of the most popular institutions of the kind in the state. Its affairs have always been administered with conspicuous ability, and the interests of depositors are so carefully guarded that it is not to be wondered at that the bank should stand exceptionally high in the confidence of the public. That this confidence is fully justified by the character of the present management, the annexed list of officers and trustees will show: President, Henry B. Noyes; Vice-President, Lemuel Clift; Secretary and Treasurer, A. H. Simmons.

Trustees.

A. H. Simmons,   Isaac D. Clift,
John O. Fish,   John A. Rathburn,
Benjamin Burrows,

Mystic River National Bank, F. M. Manning, president; Henry B. Noyes, cashier. No student of American history needs to be told that the past 40 years have seen many a serious financial panic sweep over the country, and no man in active business life during any considerable portion of that time should need to be reminded of how much the community owe to the various National banks in different sections of the union, which gave practical proof on such occasions of the firm reliance placed in the resources and integrity of the nation. It is not necessary however to go outside this state, or even outside this town to find institutions which have been tried and not been found wanting, for few if any of our New England banks have a better record in this respect than that held by the Mystic River National bank, which was incorporated as a state bank in 1851 and was re-organized under the national banking laws in 1864. This institution has been of incalculable aid in the development of the interests of this section, and will doubtless render yet more efficient help in the future, for it is constantly gaining in the confidence of the business community, and is unquestionably better prepared than ever before to offer first-class banking facilities to its patrons. The officers and directors are not only deeply interested in the prosperity of local enterprises but are in a position to render intelligent judgment concerning the needs of such, and that they have both the desire and the ability to discharge their duties satisfactorily, will we think be conceded by all. The president is Mr. F. M. Manning; cashier, Mr. Henry B. Noyes, and the directors are Messrs. F. M. Manning, Henry B. Noyes, George Greenman, Isaac W. Denison, John O. Fish, Isaac D. Holmes, Peter E. Rowland.

H. N. Wheeler, Druggist. Mystic River, Conn.—It may seem a strange assertion to make to say that the carrying on of a large number of drug stores argues well for the public health, but still there is ground for such a statement, for the simple reason that many drugs depend greatly upon their freshness for their effect, and the existence of a large number of drug stores has the result of causing each dealer to carry but a comparatively small stock of any one article; the consequence being that physicians can depend upon having their prescriptions filled by the use of ingredients much fresher than would otherwise be possible—a fact which we commend to the consideration of the few who think that now, as formerly, every doctor should furnish and compound his own medicines. Probably one of the oldest established drug stores in this section of the state is that conducted by Mr. H. N. Wheeler, for this was opened in 1846 by Mr. F. M. Manning, the present proprietor assuming possession in 1882. He is a native of this town, and has a large circle of friends throughout this vicinity. The premises measure 23 x 40 feet, and are conveniently fitted-up, special attention being given to the facilities for the accurate compounding of prescriptions at short notice. A well chosen assortment of fresh and pure drugs, medicines and chemicals is always on hand, and very reasonable charges are made in this important department. Mr. Wheeler also deals in fancy and toilet articles, window glass, pocket cutlery, and other useful goods, and is prepared to meet all honorable competition, offering strictly reliable articles at the lowest market rates.

___

Hoxie House Grocery, Fine Groceries. Teas, Coffees and Cigars, Also a Full Line of Stationery and School Supplies; Hoxie House Block, Mystic Bridge, Conn.—The "Hoxie House Grocery" needs no introduction to such of our readers as reside in Mystic Bridge and vicinity, for this enterprise was inaugurated some 13 years ago, and has become more widely and favorably known to the public with every succeeding year. Business was begun by Mr. W. E. Dickinson in 1877, and in 1888, Mr. I. C. Hoxie became proprietor, but Mr. Dickinson is still identified with the undertaking in the capacity of manager. The premises occupied are located in Hoxie House Block, and have an area of 1,500 square feet, exclusive of the storeroom and a spacious basement. The stock on hand is very extensive, and it would be difficult to find a more desirable assortment of staple and fancy groceries for family use, for Mr. Dickinson has carefully studied the requirements of his patrons during the 13 years he has catered to them, and spares no pains to fully satisfy all varieties of taste. The teas and coffees offered are of exceptionally fine and delicate flavor, and many popular brands of cigars are also on hand to choose from. A full line of stationery and school supplies is a very attractive feature, especially as the prices on these and all the other goods handled are in strict accordance with the very lowest market rates.

Allen Avery & Co., Dealers in Furniture, Mattresses and Bedding, 52 Main Street, Mystic, Conn.—While it would be foolish to deny that furniture—taken as a whole —is to-day cheaper than ever before, it would also be foolish to deny that there is a larger quantity of "trash" in the market than was the case when higher prices ruled. Now, this trash is not always distinguished by the eye by any means, for the skilful use of paint, varnish and glue will serve to cover up defects of material and workmanship, and hence it is obvious that the only way to be sure of getting dependable goods is to patronize a dependable establishment, and we may say right here that the entire state does not contain one more thoroughly deserving of being so described than that conducted by Messrs. Allen Avery & Co. The residents of Mystic River and vicinity have had ample opportunity to find this out, for the enterprise was started a quarter of a century ago. it having been inaugurated by Mr. Allen Avery in 1864. The present firm was formed in 1887, and is constituted of Messrs. Allen Avery and Frank Smith, the former being a native of Stonington, and the latter of Groton. The premises utilized comprise 3 floors, each measuring 23 x 90 feet, and no room is wasted at that, for a very extensive and complete stock is carried, including furniture of all kinds, mattresses and house furnishings in general. The firm are prepared to quote prices that will compare very favorably with those named by any dealers in goods of equal merit, and customers may implicitly rely upon the representations made, for every article is fully guaranteed to prove precisely as described.

___

H. C. Bridgham, Jeweler: Dealer in Fancy Goods and Stationery, Mystic River, Conn.— Fashions in jewelry are constantly changing, and a dealer has to keep a sharp eye on the market if he proposes to keep up with the times in every department of his business, while considerable experience is also necessary to the attainment of the best possible results, for it is only experience which fits a man to choose such goods as will be entirely satisfactory to his customers. Well, Mr. H. C. Bridgham does not lack experience at all events, for it is over a score of years since he began operations in this town, and as for his "keeping up to the times," we fancy a careful inspection of his stock will result in that question being finally and satisfactorily settled. Mr. Bridgham was born in Middletown, Ct., and has many friends in this section of the state. His store has an area of 1,000 square feet, and contains a highly attractive assortment of American and foreign watches, jewelry, optical goods, fancy goods, stationery, etc., comprising a number of late and pleasing novelties, as well as the more staple goods with which all are familiar. Mr. Bridgham quotes moderate prices in every department of his business, but offers special inducements to purchasers of watches in gold, silver or nickel cases. Repairing of all kinds is done in the most workmanlike manner, and orders can be filled at very short notice.

E. B. Noyes, Dealer in Foreign and Domestic Dry Goods, Mystic River, Conn.—The high esteem in which the establishment conducted by Mr. E. B. Noyes is held by the residents of Mystic River and vicinity, is the legitimate result of about 18 years' endeavor to keep good faith with customers in every respect, for since Mr. Noyes began operations here in 1872, he has spared no pains to afford practical evidence of the fact that he considers the interests of patrons as identical with his own. He deals largely in foreign and domestic dry goods, small wares, etc., and quotes the lowest market rates on all the many articles handled. The premises made use of have an area of about 1,800 square feet, and the stock on hand is proportionately large, being complete in every department, and comprising the very latest fashionable novelties, as well as a full selection of more staple goods. Mr. Noyes is a native of Stonington, Ct., and has a large circle of friends throughout this vicinity. He is a very careful buyer, and his customers, of course, profit by his ability in this direction, for it assures the offering of desirable goods only, and enables bottom prices to be quoted. Employment is given to 2 assistants, and callers are served promptly and courteously at all times.

Edwin Gray, Dealer in Groceries, Provisions, Fruit, etc., Morgan's Block, Main Street, West Side, Mystic River, Conn.—The establishment carried on by Mr. Edwin Gray, in Morgan's block, Main st., is, without doubt, one of the most widely and favorably known in this section, for it held a high reputation when under the control of Mr. B. W. Morgan, the original proprietor, and this reputation has been added to by Mr. Gray since he came into possession in 1888. He is a native of Ledyard, Ct., and is thoroughly acquainted with the many details of the grocery and provision business, as is proved by the exceptional success thus far met with in his present undertaking. The premises utilized are 25 x 70 feet in dimensions, and contain as carefully chosen a stock as can be found in town. It comprises choice staple and fancy groceries, provisions, fruits, vegetables, etc., and is made up of goods selected expressly for family trade. Mr. Gray quotes the lowest market rates in every department of his business, and employs sufficient assistance to enable prompt and careful attention to be given to every customer.

Mrs. K. D. Sawyer, Dealer in Millinery, Ladies' Underwear and Fancy Goods, Mystic River, Conn.—The establishment carried on by Mrs. K. D. Sawyer caters exclusively to the gentler sex, for the stock on hand is made up of goods designed expressly for their use, and so skilfully has it been selected that we doubt if a more desirable assortment can be found in this section of the state. Mrs. Sawyer only began operations in 1886, but her store has already become an established favorite among the most discriminating buyers, not only on account of the attractiveness of the stock carried, but also by reason of the exquisite taste and skill shown in the doing of custom millinery work. Employment is given to 2 assistants during the season, and a most enviable reputation has been built up for delivering orders promptly when promised. Trimmed and untrimmed hats and bonnets are largely dealt in, together with laces, silks, satins, ribbons, flowers, feathers, ornaments, etc., and ladies' underwear and fancy goods are also extensively handled. Moderate prices are quoted, and the latest and most fashionable novelties are sure to be found at this deservedly popular store.

S. H. Buckley, Dealer in Choice Beef, Mutton, Lamb, Veal, Pork, etc., Main Street, Mystic River, Conn.—It is perfectly safe to assume that practically all of our readers will be interested in the establishment of which Mr. S. H. Buckley is the proprietor, located on Main st., for nearly everybody is fond of good meats, and is desirous of finding a place where a large assortment of such is kept, and where the lowest market rates are quoted right along. Mr. Buckley is a native of England, and founded his present business nearly 30 years ago, operations having been begun in 1860. The premises utilized are 19 x 50 feet in dimensions, and are fitted up with all necessary facilities, enabling orders to be filled without delay notwithstanding the magnitude of the business. No trouble is spared to keep the stock complete in every department, and choice beef, mutton, lamb, veal, pork, etc., are always on hand in sufficient quantity and variety to admit of all tastes being suited. Mr. Buckley employs 2 efficient assistants, and insists upon equally prompt and polite attention being given every customer, large or small. His prices are as low as the lowest, quality considered, and the goods may be depended on to prove just as represented.

Randall Browne, River Side Ice Cream Garden, Foreign and Domestic Fruits, Choice Confectionery, etc., Mystic River, Conn.—If we were asked to compile a list of the most popular establishments located in Mystic River and the adjoining sections, we would certainly give the enterprise carried on by Mr. Randall Browne prominent place among them, for the "River Side Ice Cream Garden," as this establishment is sometimes called, is not only very largely patronized now, but is gaining rapidly and steadily in the favor of the public. Mr. Browne was born in Mystic Bridge, and began his present business in 1875. He deals in foreign and domestic fruits, fine confectionery, bread, cake and pastry, and spares no pains to handle only such goods as he has reason to believe will give the best of satisfaction. The ice cream sold here is famous even in this section (where it is said the best ice cream in the state is made), and this enviable reputation is in no danger of being lost if careful selection of material and the observance of other precautions can maintain it. Employment is given to 2 efficient assistants, and every customer is sure of receiving immediate and painstaking attention, low prices being quoted in every department of the business.

Roswell Brown & Son, Hack, Livery and Boarding Stables, Mystic River, Conn.—No matter what a man has to sell—whether it be flour, sugar or anything else—he best serves his own interests by making a practice of giving his customers the full worth of their money. Temporary success may be gained by imposition sometimes, but all trade is dependent on both parties being benefitted, and neither can thrive long at the expense of the other. The exceptionally high reputation, held by the enterprise conducted by Messrs. Roswell Brown & Son, is directly due to this fact, for during the many years that this undertaking has been carried on, the invariable policy pursued has been to render a fair equivalent for every dollar received. Mr. Roswell Brown is a native of North Stonington, and founded his present business some 40 years ago. In 1883, the existing firm was formed, Mr. James E. F. Brown, a native of Groton, being admitted to partnership. The senior partner has held various town offices of trust, and is one of the most widely and favorably known of our local business men, while his son also has many friends, and shows great enterprise in catering to the steadily increasing list of patrons. The firm maintain extensive and well-equipped hack, livery and boarding stables, there being 24 stalls on the premises, and employment being given to 3 competent assistants. Carriages are run daily to and from the railroad station, at all hours of day or night, and passengers and baggage will be transported at very reasonable rates. First-class single and double teams will be furnished at short notice, and carriages for funerals, weddings and parties will also be supplied, together with experienced and careful drivers. The stables have telephonic communication, and all orders are assured prompt and painstaking attention, moderate prices being quoted in every department of the business.

J. H. Alexander, S. D.: Teeth Extracted and Artificial Teeth Made; Pure Nitrous Oxide Gas Administered; Mystic River, Conn.—The older residents of Mystic River and vicinity do not need to be reminded of the facilities possessed by Mr. J. H. Alexander for the practice of surgeon dentistry in all its branches, for this gentleman has carried on his profession here for very nearly a quarter of a century, and his reputation for doing skilful, thorough and durable work is the legitimate result of the methods employed during this extended period. But this book will pass into the hands of many who are strangers or comparative strangers in this vicinity, and as some of these may very probably have occasion for the services of an experienced and competent dentist, we take pleasure in calling their attention to the advantages Mr. Alexander is prepared to offer. The premises occupied comprise a reception room, a laboratory and an office, and are very conveniently fitted up, the latest improved apparatus being utilized, and operations being carried on in accordance with the most approved methods. Pure nitrous oxide gas will be administered if desired, and the most difficult teeth can thus be extracted without pain. Gold, Silver and other fillings will be inserted in a neat and permanent manner at moderate rates, and artificial teeth will be made to order, all work being fully warranted.

B. W. Morgan, dealer in Provisions, Vegetables, Butter, Fresh and Salt Meats of all kinds, Flour at the lowest prices; Mystic River, Conn.—There is one kind of information that is always in demand, and that is, anything relating to where dependable meats and provisions may be obtained at low rates. Therefore no apology is necessary for calling the attention of our readers to the establishment conducted by Mr. B. W. Morgan, for reliable meats and other family supplies may be found here if anywhere and the prices quoted are as low as the lowest in every instance. Mr. Morgan is a native of Stonington, and served in the army during the Rebellion. He began operations in this town about a score of years ago, and up to 1888 dealt in general merchandise, but since that date has confined himself to handling meats and provisions, including fresh and salt meats of all kinds, butter, vegetables, etc. Mr. Morgan has lately put in a new track for the purpose of handling grades of beef which he buys in large quantities, owing to his extensive trade. Mr. Morgan employs 3 efficient and courteous assistants, and every caller is assured immediate attention, orders being promptly and accurately delivered.

Mrs. A. J. Holdridge, dealer in Millinery and Fancy Goods, also Worsteds, Madame Foy's Corset Skirt Supporters, etc., Holdridge Block, Mystic River, Conn.—It is inevitable that in every community there should be establishments which, either on account of their long standing, the excellence of the service provided, or both, should be universally conceded to be the leaders in their particular line, and among such it is fitting that prominent mention should be made of that conducted by Mrs. A. J. Holdridge, in Holdridge Block, for this business was founded in 1861 and has been classed among the truly representative enterprises of this section for a full score of years, Mrs. Holdridge is a native of Mystic, and has a very large circle of friends throughout this vicinity. Her long and varied experience is of course of great advantage to her in the filling of orders for fine millinery work, and as her taste is exceptionally correct it is not surprising that no difficulty should be met with in satisfying the most fastidious customers. The store is 15 x 50 feet in dimensions, and contains a beautiful stock of millinery and fancy goods comprising the very latest fashionable novelties, for Mrs. Holdridge keeps thoroughly well-informed concerning the dictates of fashion and makes it a rule to give her patrons the earliest possible chance to select from the most approved styles; worsteds, small wares, etc., are also dealt in to a considerable extent and uniformly moderate rates are quoted on all the articles handled.

P. A. Noyes, dealer in Groceries, Provisions, Fruit, Vegetables, etc., Mystic River, Conn.—Although some people seem to think that anybody can carry on a grocery and provision store successfully, they have only to use their eyes and ears in order to ascertain how incorrect such a belief is, for many who open such establishments fail altogether, and still more only manage to "keep along" and cannot honestly be said to have succeeded at all. But of course there are stores which are successful in every sense of the word and among these may be classed that conducted by Mr. P. A. Noyes, for although but recently opened it has already attained great popularity, and the inducements offered are sure to steadily increase the trade. Mr. Noyes was born in Stonington, and has been engaged in his present line of business in this town for some 12 or 15 years, opening his present store in 1889. It is 30 x 50 feet in dimensions, affording plenty of room for the carrying of a large and varied stock of choice staple and fancy groceries, provisions, fruits, vegetables, etc. The goods are first-class, the prices are low, and the service is prompt and polite so there is little reason to wonder at the liberal patronage bestowed upon the establishment. The public know that articles bought here are sure to prove just as represented and show their appreciation by giving very liberal support to the enterprise.

Chas. H. Brooks, Fresh and Salt Meats, Poultry and Game, Vegetables in season, Main Street, Ryan's Block. Mystic River, Conn.— It would doubtless surprise even some of the older residents of this section to learn the amount of fresh meat that is consumed here every day, but the number and character of the retail establishments devoted to supplying this demand form a significant indication that the total amount must be very large. But among them all, it is safe to assert that not one is more widely and favorably known than that conducted by Mr. Charles H. Brooks, in Ryan's Block, Main Street, for the "Bridge Market," as this store is called, is managed on liberal principles and has built up its present prosperity on the same ground of entire satisfaction to every reasonable customer. The proprietor is a native of New York state and inaugurated the enterprise in 1885. The premises are 20 x 50 feet in dimensions, and at all times contain an attractive and seasonable stock, comprising fresh and salted meats, poultry, game, vegetables, fruit, butter, eggs, etc. Mr. Brooks caters to all classes of trade and strives to make it for his customers' interests to place all their orders with him. He quotes the lowest market rates and sells every article under a guarantee that it will prove just as represented.

Geo. A. Perkins, Dealer in Clothing and Gent's Furnishings, Hats and Caps, No. 4 Ryan's Block, Mystic River. Conn.—We may safely take it for granted that our readers are interested in the subject of clothing, for practically everybody who amounts to anything is careful of his personal appearance, and, of course, this is influenced to a great measure by the character of the clothing worn. There are a number of establishments in this vicinity where clothing may be bought to excellent advantage, and it would be the height of folly to assert that any particular one must be patronized in order to get fashionable and well-made garments at reasonable rates, but still in this business as in others, some dealers offer special inducements, and we have no hesitation in saying that Mr. George A. Perkins should be classed with these, for we are confident that a visit to his store, at No. 4 Ryan's block, will result in this assertion being confirmed by every competent judge who may give him a call. Mr. Perkins was born in Hope Valley, Rhode Island, and began operations here in 1888. The premises utilized measure 20 x 60 feet, and afford sufficient room for the accommodation of a very complete assortment of clothing and gent's furnishings, together with an attractive stock of hats, caps, etc. The latest fashionable novelties are well represented, and the prices are as low as can be quoted in connection with equally desirable goods. Mr. Perkins gives personal attention to customers, and spares no pains to entirely satisfy the most fastidious.

W. E. Wheeler, Dealer in Dry Goods, Groceries, Provisions, Hardware, Grain, Flour, Feed, etc., Mystic River, Conn.—In referring to the establishment carried on by Mr. W. E. Wheeler, it is necessary to speak in general terms only, for the magnitude of the business and the variety and completeness of the stock are so great that anything like detailed mention would exhaust the limits of available space many times over. This business was founded by Messrs. William E. Wheeler & Son in 1868, and has been under the sole control of the present proprietor for about 14 years. It holds a leading position among all enterprises of a similar nature in this section, and is certainly deserving of its popularity, for this has been won by strictly legitimate methods, and is maintained by continued efforts to serve the public to the best possible advantage. The premises occupied comprise 2 floors of the dimensions of 56 x 60 feet, and the very heavy stock on hand is so arranged as to enable all orders to be filled with promptness and accuracy. It is made up of dry goods, groceries, provisions, etc., together with a full assortment of hardware, while grain, flour, feed, etc., are also very largely represented. Mr. Wheeler makes it a rule to sell every article strictly on its merits, so that it is almost unnecessary to add that all goods are guaranteed to prove as represented, and fills orders at short notice.

Hoxie House Hack, Livery, Boarding and Feed Stable, A. G. Brownell, Prop'r; First-Class Single and Double Teams to Let: Mystic Bridge, Conn.—The Hoxie House Livery, Hack, Boarding and Feed Stable has been in charge of the present proprietor, Mr. A. G. Brownell, ever since 1874, and during that time has gained a leading position among the most popular public stables in this section. Those conversant with Mr. Brownell's methods, will agree with us that this is only what was naturally to be expected, for the majority of the public are sure to appreciate liberal and intelligent service, and it would be difficult to find more thoroughly satisfactory accommodations than those furnished at this well-managed establishment. The premises are 45 x 70 feet in dimensions, and are kept in the best of condition, every facility being at hand for the proper care of horses, which will be taken to board at very reasonable rates. A number of first-class single and double teams are on hand for livery purposes, and orders can be filled at very short notice, moderate rates being quoted in every instance. Passengers and baggage will be carried to or from the depot, all orders for such service left at the stable, being assured prompt and painstaking attention.

T. E. Packer & Co., Real Estate and Insurance Agents, Bank Building, Up Stairs, Mystic Bridge, Conn.—The insurance agency, conducted by Messrs. T. E. Packer & Co., is one of the oldest established as it is one of the best known in this section of the state, and the character of the service afforded during the many years that operations have been carried on, is significantly shown by the unlimited confidence expressed by some of our most conservative business men in the integrity and ability of the management. The enterprise was inaugurated by Mr. Charles H. Denison, he being succeeded by Messrs. Denison & Packer in 1865. Mr. T. E. Packer afterwards became sole proprietor, and finally the present firm was formed,—this consisting of Messrs. T. E. Packer and Frank W. Batty, both of whom are natives of Groton, Ct. Some of the strongest insurance corporations in the world are represented, as, for instance, the North British and Mercantile, the Ætna, of Hartford, the Franklin, of Philadelphia, and many others, and the firm are in a position to write policies at the very lowest market rates on thoroughly dependable insurance. The of-

fice is located in the bank building, up stairs, and all desired information will cheerfully be given on application. This firm also transacts a general real-estate and loan business, and has some very desirable property for sale or to let. Western investment securities of all kinds are dealt in extensively.

Thos. H. Newbury, House and Ship Plumber, Tin, Copper and Sheet Iron Worker and Dealer in Stoves, Ranges, Hardware, Guns, Ammunition, Fishing Tackle, House Furnishing goods, etc. Mystic Bridge, Conn.—The premises utilized by Mr. Thomas H. Newbury, comprise three floors of the dimensions of 25x 65 feet, one floor being used as a salesroom, another as a workshop, and the third as a storeroom. Mr. Newbury is a native of New London, Conn., and is one of the best-known of our local business men, having founded his

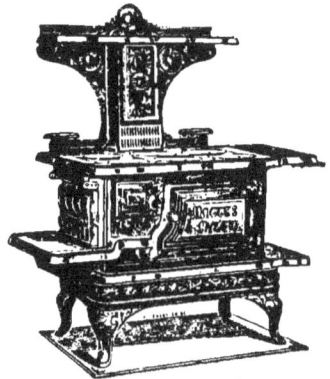

present undertaking over a score of years ago. He is a House and Ship Plumber, and is prepared to fill orders for Tin, Copper and Sheet Iron work at short notice, while he deals extensively in Stoves, Ranges, Hardware, Crockery and House Furnishing Goods, as well as in Guns, Pistols, Ammunition and Fishing Tackle, The prices quoted are always in strict accordance with the lowest market rates, for Mr. Newbury enjoys the most favorable relations with producers and wholesalers and makes it a point to meet all honorable competition. Employment is given to from 5 to 12 assistants, and order work can always be promptly and satisfactorily attended to. The prime necessity of having Plumbing done in the best possible manner is becoming very generally understood, for the newspapers daily contain accounts of the evil consequences of incompetency or carelessness in the doing of such work. It is well worth while to take a few precautions to ensure good health in the family, and such Plumbing as that done under Mr. Newbury's direction will go far towards bringing about that desirable result.

Geo. D. Packer, Insurance, Real Estate and Loan Agent, Buckley's Block, Mystic River, Conn.—It is not so very long since it was considered immoral in some quarters to insure anything, the argument being that worldly affairs were bound to be uncertain, and man had no business to try to change such a condition of affairs. People, of course, smile at such a claim nowadays, but it is only by recalling it that an adequate idea of the wonderful development of the insurance business can be gained. The agency, now conducted by Mr. George D. Packer, was founded over a score of years ago by Hon. William H. Potter, and the high record it has made for enterprise and fair dealing, together with the greatly increased demand for insurance, have combined to develop its business to large proportions. The present proprietor is a native of New York city, and is widely known in business circles hereabouts in connection with the placing of insurance in standard companies. He represents many such, both stock and mutual, and can write policies at as low rates as are obtainable on trustworthy insurance. But "the proof of the pudding is in the eating," and the proof of the above statements is to be found in the character and magnitude of Mr. Packer's business, and in the following list of companies represented:

Continental,	New York.
German American.	"
Niagara,	"
Westchester,	"
Hartford,	Hartford.
Connecticut,	"
Lancashire,	England.
Commercial Union,	"
Norwich Union,	"
Security.	New Haven.
Mutual Companies.	
Hartford County,	Hartford.
State Mutual,	"
New London County,	Norwich.

Mr. Packer also transacts a real estate and Western loan business, being agent for this section for the Jarvis-Conklin Mortgage Trust Company of Kansas City.

F. B. Smith, Plumber, Steam and Gas fitter. Tinware, Tin, Copper and Sheet Iron Worker, Dealer in Richmond Stoves, Ranges and Furnaces, Pumps, Sinks, Lead and Iron Pipe, etc., Avery's Block, Mystic Bridge, Conn.—As a general thing, it is almost as essential to have orders for plumbing filled at short notice as it is to have the work thoroughly and skilfully done, for the majority of such orders are in the line of Repairing, and "delays are dangerous" where plumbing is concerned. For this reason if no other, the service afforded by Mr F. B. Smith is sure to win much commendation in the future as it has in the past, for a specialty is made of filling orders at short notice and the work is done honestly as well as promptly. Mr. Smith is a native of Long Island and is very generally known in this vicinity. He has carried on his present establishment in Avery's Block since 1887, having at that time succeeded Mr. Parmenas Avery. The premises measure 25x50 feet, exclusive of a good size store room, and a large stock is on hand at all times, for Mr. Smith deals extensively in Tinware, Kitchen Furnishings, Richmond Stoves, Ranges and Furnaces. Pumps, Sinks, Lead and Iron Pipe, etc. Employment is given to 2 assistants, and Tin, Copper and Sheet Iron work of all descriptions will be done in first-class style at moderate rates. Steam and Gas Fitting are also given prompt and satisfactory attention and no trouble is spared to fully maintain the enviable reputation thus far held.

Schofield & Tingley, Artistic Photographers, Mystic River, also New London. Good work as low as the lowest. Children's Pictures a specialty. Office hours from 9 A. M. to 4 P. M.—When deciding where to place orders for anything in the photographic line, the first point to be considered is the character of the work done, for although good photographs are sometimes charged for at somewhat exhorbitant rates, one is better satisfied under such circumstances than when furnished with poor pictures at a very much lower figure. But as a matter of fact, there is not the least necessity for paying fancy prices in order to get thoroughly artistic work, and the proof of this statement may be found at the establishments conducted by Messrs. Schofield & Tingley; one being located at No. 59 State Street, New London, and the other in this town. This firm announce that they are prepared to supply good work as low as the lowest, and no competent and unprejudiced judge can examine the photographs and note the prices quoted on them, without conceding that this announcement is fully justified by the facts. This business was founded by Mr. E. A. Schofield about a score of years ago, and the existing co-partnership was formed in 1886. Mr. Schofield is a native of Lowell, Mass., while Mr. George E. Tingley was born in Mystic, Conn. It is unnecessary for us to eulogize the results attained at this popular studio, for the public are generally familiar with the uniform excellence of the work, and a cordial invitation is constantly extended to all interested to call and see for themselves. A specialty is made of children's pictures, and the most improved facilities are at hand for the carrying on of photography in all its branches. Office hours are from 9 a. m. to 4 p. m., and every caller is assured immediate and polite attention.

G. E. T. Ward, D. D. S., Dental Parlors, Opera House Block; Office Hours, 8 a. m. to 5 p. m.; Mystic, Conn.—It doesn't pay to abuse any portion of the body, least of all the teeth, and that the public are beginning to appreciate the fact is proved by the increased attention given to the care and preservation of these highly important tools, for after all, the teeth are chiefly tools to aid in preparing the food for the stomach, and like all other tools, they must be kept in good condition if they are to do good work. The practice of submitting them to the inspection of a competent and reliable dentist at reasonably frequent intervals is highly to be commended, for when this is done, incipient decay or any other destructive tendency can be arrested at the start, and much irreparable injury prevented. In this connection, we may properly call attention to the facilities possessed by G. E. T. Ward, D. D. S., for this gentleman is one of the most conscientious and skilful dentists known to us, and his dental parlors, in Opera House block, are fitted up with the very latest improved tools and appliances, thus enabling operations to be carried on to the best possible advantage, and at the least possible inconvenience to patients. Dr. Ward was born in this town, and is a graduate of the New York college of dentistry. He only opened his present rooms in 1889, but the residents of this vicinity have had ample opportunity to become practically acquainted with his methods, as he has practiced his profession here for about 5 years. That the result of such acquaintance is distinctly favorable, is evident from the active demand for his services, and this popularity is due not only to the popular conviction that Dr. Ward is thoroughly competent, but also to the gentleness which characterizes his methods. His office hours are from 8 a. m. to 5 p. m., and appointments may be made in advance, thus obviating uncertainty.

J. L. Manning & Co., Grain, Meal and Feed; (Mill at Mystic); Mystic Bridge.—The enterprise conducted by Messrs. J. L. Manning & Co. was inaugurated a good many years ago, the present proprietors succeeding Messrs. Chipman & Co. in 1875. This undertaking is worthy of particularly prominent mention, not only by reason of its own intrinsic importance, but also on account of the leading position held by individual members of the firm among those most active in developing the interests of this section, they being very prominently identified with the two national banks, Mr. F. M. Manning being president of both. The firm is composed of Messrs. J. L. Manning, F. M. Manning and H. B. Noyes, all of whom are natives of Mystic. An extensive wholesale and retail business is done in grain, meal, feed, etc., the storehouse being located at Mystic Bridge—where the vessels are unloaded—while the mill is in Mystic. It is run by water-power, and is of sufficient capacity to allow of all orders being promptly and satisfactorily filled. The store is 22 x 72 feet in dimensions, and always contains a large and varied stock, the quality of the commodities comprised within it being fully guaranteed, while the prices quoted are always in strict accordance with the lowest market rates.

Waterman's Pharmacy, Mystic Bridge, Conn.—If the comparative rank of a business is to be judged from its usefulness to the community, the undertaking conducted by Mr. J. W. Waterman must be given a leading position, for "Waterman's Pharmacy" is without doubt at least as useful an establishment as this section can show, and it is very thoroughly appreciated by the public in general. It has been under the control of the present proprietor since 1884, he succeeded at that date Messrs. H. B. Noyes & Co. The store is 22x50 feet in dimensions and is very completely fitted-up with all necessary facilities for the handling and storage of the large stock of Drugs, Medicines and Chemicals which is constantly carried, for Mr. Waterman makes a specialty of the compounding of prescriptions, and spares no pains to assure prompt and absolute accuracy. Sufficient assistance is employed to enable immediate attention to be given to every caller, and a carefully chosen assortment of Toilet and Fancy Goods etc., is always on hand, the latest novelties being represented and uniformly moderate prices quoted. Mr. Waterman has enjoyed a long experience in the business.

FIRST NATIONAL BANK,

MYSTIC BRIDGE, CT.

Capital, $150,000.

PRESIDENT,

F. M. MANNING.

CASHIER.

E. P. RANDALL.

DIRECTORS.

F. M. MANNING,
GEO. GREENMAN,
GURDON GATES,
E. P. RANDALL,
GEO. H. GREENMAN

LEADING BUSINESS MEN OF ASHAWAY, R. I.

T. A. Barbor, Druggist. Dealer in Boots and Shoes, Wall Paper, Oil Cloths, Books, Stationery, Jewelry, etc., Holiday Goods in their season. Ashaway, R. I.—An establishment in which the residents of Ashaway and vicinity put the utmost confidence is that conducted by Mr. T. A. Barbor, and indeed it would be strange if this enterprise did not stand high in the public esteem for it has been carried on for a long period and has been liberally as well as intelligently managed from the very first. Mr. Barbor began operations across the river about a score of years ago, and erected the building he now occupies in 1877. The store is spacious and well arranged, and the stock is worthy of much more extended mention than the limits of our space will allow us to give it as it includes not only a complete assortment of drugs, medicines and chemicals, but also a full line of footwear, comprising boots, shoes, rubbers etc., in the latest and most approved designs. The facilities for the prompt and accurate compounding of physicians' prescriptions are sufficiently ample to enable all such orders to be filled at very short notice and great care is exercised in every detail of the work, rendering serious error practically impossible. Mr. Barbor handles the productions of some of the leading shoe manufacturers of the country and is in a position to give unsurpassed values to his customers. He is thoroughly familiar with the requirements of local trade and his assortment is so carefully selected and so varied that it is safe to say all tastes can be suited from it. Callers are given prompt and painstaking attention, and polite treatment is assured to all, goods being cheerfully shown and no pains being spared to enable every patron to choose intelligently and satisfactorily, while all articles are guaranteed to prove just as represented in every respect. Mr. Barbor also makes a specialty of holiday goods which he opens about December 1st. These embrace all varieties and the assortment is offered at prices which will suit all tastes and purses. They are purchased direct of the large Boston and New York jobbers and importers and he guarantees his prices in every case to be as low as the lowest, quality considered.

G. B. Langworthy, General Store, Ashaway, R. I.—When reviewing establishments at which a specialty is made of a certain line of goods—as for instance, a clothing store, a shoe store, a dry goods store, etc.,—it is comparatively easy to give a somewhat detailed description of the stock as it is confined to narrow limits and can therefore be summarized quite readily, but when mentioning such an undertaking as that carried on by Mr. G. B. Langworthy, any detailed description is quite out of the question for the simple reason that such a varied assortment is carried that a mere catalogue of the goods composing it would cover several pages. Mr. Langworthy deals in groceries, meats, provisions and general merchandise and caters to all classes of trade so, as may well be imagined, his stock is especially large and varied. One thing may be said however of *all* the goods comprised within it—they will prove as represented every time. A large and constantly growing business is done, and the particularly close attention given to family trade has resulted in the building up of a very heavy patronage in this line alone. Sufficient assistance is employed to assure prompt and careful attention to every caller, and the prices quoted on the many commodities handled will always be found to accord strictly with the lowest market rates.

Philip Rexroth. Fish Dealer, Ashaway, R. I.—There is of course an enormous quantity of fish sold every year, but it is safe to assert that a very much larger quantity could be disposed of were certain dealers more painstaking in their methods. Fish to be good must be perfectly fresh, and it is on account of the difficulty they experience in obtaining such that many families make very little use of this article of diet. Mr. Philip Rexroth has carried on a fish market here in Ashaway for about five years and has built up a very desirable trade, a great part of which is directly due to his policy of so frequently renewing his stock as to always have it fresh and attractive in every department. Of course the prices had to be about right too, but Mr. Rexroth experienced no difficulty on that score, for he is thoroughly acquainted with the many details of his business and is prepared to meet all honorable competition; quoting the lowest market rates on all the commodities he handles. During the summer months Mr. Rexroth handles large quantities of poultry, supplying the principal hotels and cottages at Watch Hill. The stock of fish varies greatly with the season of course but will always be found well worthy of inspection as it is kept as full as possible in every department. Fresh and salt water fish, oysters and clams, lobsters, etc., are among the principal varieties dealt in, and smoked, salted and pickled fish are also handled extensively, orders being filled at short notice and at bottom rates.

HISTORICAL SKETCH

OF

NOANK.

Noank is a part of the old and widely famed town of Groton, with which its history and progress have been intimately connected from the beginning. The entire town of Groton comprises several villages including Noank, Pequonnock and Groton village, and covers about six square miles of territory. The land is mostly uneven and hilly, the higher land not being very fertile but containing in some places very fine ledges of granite, the output of the quarries of the town being widely famed for its high qualities of beauty and durability. Through the many pleasant villages of the town are fertile areas and many quiet and beautiful farms, the leading agricultural interest being dairy farming. The forests of the town are also remarkably well preserved, and add to the beauty and salubrity of the region.

The history of the town, in which the citizens of Noank have shared and taken an active part, has been one of the most stirring in the annals of the state. The town was first incorporated in 1705, among the earliest in the state, but before that time the region had occupied a conspicious place in colonial history. This was the ancient seat and center of the Pequot Indians, the race that gave more trouble to the early colonists of Connecticut than any other. Hither the whole tribe was driven back and concentrated in 1637, when Capt. Mason led the colonial militia against them and on this spot was fought one of the bloodiest battles in colonial history. A large part of the Indian forces was destroyed and the Pequot tribe as a distinct body of Indians annihilated; so that they ceased to be a source of trouble and anxiety thereafter. The memory of this bloody event lingered long throughout New England and perhaps was one reason why at first this section was not so rapidly settled as some others, but after King Philip's war in 1675 it made steady progress in population and prosperity. Noank in the south-western part of the town was one of the earliest sections to be settled and built up, its good harbor being early utilized by the fishing and other nautical interests that began to spring up after the middle of the eighteenth century. During the Revolutionary war the citizens took

an earnest, patriotic part in the various calls upon their exertions and resources
that were made, and especially distinguished themselves in the famous assault
of Fort Griswold, September 6, 1781, which was the bloodiest episode of the
state's history and it seemed a case of history repeating itself that it should
have occurred here, on the spot of the Pequot battle a century and a half earlier.
This assault took place during Benedict Arnold's incursion into Connecticut,
and was characterized by the exceptional animosity which he seemed to show
toward his old home region. Fort Griswold was garrisoned with one hundred
and fifty men, under the command of Col. Wm. Ledyard, one of the heroic type
of men, who, though the British troops which landed to storm the fort about
9 a. m., Sept. 6, 1781, were eight hundred strong determined to fight it
out, though outnumbered five to one. For several hours the fight raged fierce-
ly, the British at first suffering heavily and losing their commanding officer
Major Montgomery. Finally by mere force of numbers the British drove back
the little band of heroes and swarmed over the breast works with the cry "put
every man to death; don't spare one." Seeing resistance out of the question,
Col. Ledyard surrendered his sword to the leader of the British, who, contrary
to all rules of war and dictates of humanity, immediately ran him through the
body with it. Then followed a general massacre until every American who had
not been able to escape lay dead or dying in the little fort, which according to an
eye witness ran ankle deep with blood. Thus ended the most atrocious and
brutal battle during the war, unless we except the Wyoming Massacre, or
similar action by the red-skinned, though not red coated savages. Fifty-four
of the British were slain, and one hundred and forty-three men wounded. The
names of the eighty-five brave Americans, who stood firm for their country and
homes in the face of inevitable death and found honored patriot graves, are in-
scribed on the monument which now stands at Fort Griswold, looking over the
Thames toward New London. It is 127 feet high, ascended by an iron stair-
case within, and is one of the most conspicuous and interesting historic objects
in Connecticut. The citizens of Noank also took part in the repulse of the similar though less fatal display of British valor guided by atrocity, which marked
the bombardment of Stonington in 1814. The most serious historic event of the
first half of the present century to Noank was the decay of the shipping interests
of New England, through government interference and other unfortunate circumstances. Nevertheless the people bore up against this injury to their
dearest and most essential industry with no less fortitude than that shown in
battle, and they are now able to boast the largest ship-building establishment in
New England. The building of smaller boats, yachts and launches has greatly
developed in recent years, and this port is now one of the most famed on the
coast for this line of workmanship. In this and other ways Noank has shared
in the increasing prosperity which has come to this region of late years, through
the summer traffic which is making this one of the best-known sections of New
England and the Atlantic coast. Situated at one of the loveliest spots on the
Sound coast, with celebrated resorts near at hand, and in itself a beautiful and
attractive town, with pleasant shaded streets lined with many tasty, quiet and
handsome residences, with fine river and harbor shores, combined with rural

retreats, charming valleys, lanes and woods Noank, has not escaped the observant eye of many beauty-loving visitors to this section and though it has not sought for fame with great hotel accommodations, has not been without its portion of the summer visitation to the health restoring and enjoyable attractions of this sea-side locality — a portion which promises large increase in coming years, and needs must increase as the beauties of the town and the sterling, hospitable character of its citizens become better known.

LEADING BUSINESS MEN

OF

NOANK.

Robert Palmer & Sons, Ship Builders, and proprietors of Marine Railways, Vessels hauled out and repaired, Noank, Conn.—Noank has the honor of claiming the largest and most progressive ship-building establishment in New England. The old house of Robert Palmer & Sons has been established over forty years, and has gone steadily forward in its methods, and extent of business, while it has witnessed almost all the similar enterprises coeval with itself in point of time, succumb to the force of a hostile environment and go out of existence. But in the very energy and perseverance with which this house has overcome all the difficulties and discouragements in the way of American shipping, lies the secret of the great progress. Established by Robert and John Palmer, and conducted by Mr. Robert Palmer up to 1880, when the present firm name and co-partnership was entered upon, the spirit of the house from the first has been marked by unrivalled foresight, the utilization of every possible improvement, and the persevering conquest of every obstacle. On this solid foundation has the present extensive business been built up. The present large plant of the company has been extended gradually until it includes several acres of land and wharves, with several large buildings, and an immense marine railway capable of receiving vessels as large as the steamer Connecticut or

Rhode Island. Besides the above magnificent steamboats, the firm has also constructed the Nashua and the Block Island, besides many other smaller craft. The average employee force is about one hundred and thirty men and there are always several great vessels undergoing repairs or construction in their great ship-yards. The present firm is composed of Messrs. Robert Palmer, Robert Palmer, Jr., and S. W. Ashby. The two former are both natives of Noank and have filled with honor, seats in the Connecticut Legislature. Mr. Ashby is a native of Mystic, who, though he has never entered public life, also enjoys the high esteem of this section, throughout which the name of the firm are familiar and honored.

Robert Palmer, Jr., Boat Builder, Noank, Conn.—In 1885, Mr. Robert Palmer, Jr., of the well-known firm of R. Palmer & Sons, recognizing the demand for a special line of light craft, established as a private enterprise, a Boat-building business which has proved its *raison d'etre* (reason for existence) by the large measure of success it has achieved. A specialty has been made since the start in the building of Steam Launches, and some of the most staunch, beautiful and fast sailing craft of this sort in eastern waters, have been built here. An employee force averaging 6 or 7 expert workmen is kept constantly busied over the increasing patronage which the fine work of this house is receiving, and all who desire the best results and moderate terms in the line of Steam Launches, Yachts or Small Boats, will do well to consult Mr. R. Palmer, Jr., either at his shops at the foot of Main street, or at the office of R. Palmer & Sons, where they will receive full specifications, plans and estimates and a quality of work which can be thoroughly depended upon.

O. E. Miner & Son, Druggists, Office No. 6, Main Street, Noank, Conn.—That the requirements of the druggist's trade demand long and careful training, thorough knowledge and experience, is a fact too obvious to need demonstration, and that these qualities have been sustained by the old established house of O. E. Miner & Son, is evident from the confidence and reputation it has enjoyed for over twenty years. It was established in 1867, by O. E. Miner, M. D., and soon after his son Mr. O. E. Miner, Jr., was admitted to the firm. From the start the house has been noted for the reliability of its goods, also the carefulness of its service and its reasonable terms. It now occupies a commodious and nicely fitted up store (45x30 feet in dimensions,) and filled with a large and reliable stock of Drugs, also Fancy Goods, Confectionery, Cigars, and a well selected circulating library. Dr. Miner in addition to his medical practice is the Medical Examiner for the whole town of Groton, and both he and his son are esteemed among the most valuable and honored members of the community. An inspection of the large and finely arranged stock here presented will be sure to repay all those in need of these lines of necessary and beautiful articles.

S. B. Latham, Groceries and Provisions, Noank, Conn.—The Grocery business now conducted here by Mr. S. B. Latham is one of the best known in this vicinity. It was established in 1871, under the firm name of Latham Bros. which continued up to 1879, when Mr. S. B. Latham became proprietor and has been since. The purpose of the house since its inception has been to furnish reliable goods at the lowest market prices and the enterprising efforts of the proprietor have met with hearty appreciation from his patrons. A nice stock of family groceries and provisions will be found at this store which is neatly fitted up and about 25x40 feet in dimensions. We would advise all those desiring advantageous bargains in all lines of fine groceries to pay a visit to this established and reliable stand and they will receive courteous and careful attention. Mr. S. B. Latham is a native of New York City, and since his establishment here has gained wide respect and esteem for his straight-forward dealings as a business man, and the gentlemanly qualities of mind and heart which have secured to him many friends throughout this whole vicinity.

W. F. Chesebro, Ship, House and Sign Painter, Dealer in Paints, Oils, Varnish, Glass, Brushes, etc., Agents for the Genuine Rubber Mixed paints, all shades, prompt attention given to orders for Painting, Graining and Kalsomining, Main Street, opposite Post office, Noank, Conn.—The art of house painting and decorating has made great progress in our New England clime during the last quarter of a century, and no one has had a greater influence in extending advanced ideas in this direction throughout this region than Mr. Wm. Chesebro. His business was established here about 1863, and ever since has been steadily carried on, gaining in reputation and custom. At his shop on Main street, Mr. Chesebro carries a large and varied stock of painter's goods, including paints, oils, glass, brushes, etc., but most of the work is done to order outside. A specialty is made in the painting of yachts, for which there has been an increasing demand during recent years, and every branch of which work Mr. Chesebro performs with most careful exactitude and artistic skill and beauty. House and sign painting are also executed in a most artistic manner, as is interior decorating. The number of employees varies with the season, but on an average numbers seven. Mr. Chesebro is a native of this town and has achieved a well earned and honorable name as a business man.

R. A. Morgan, Builder of Steam Yachts, Launches, Sail and Row Boats, Noank, Conn.—Not the least of Noank's honorable boasts, is that she contains the oldest boat building establishment in this section, namely that of Mr. R. A. Morgan. It was established over sixty years ago by Mr. Roswell Morgan, who was succeeded in 1869 by Mr. R. A. Morgan, the present proprietor. During recent years the business has been conducted by Mr. J. W. Morgan, son of Mr. R. A. Morgan. The house has long had an unsurpassed reputation for strength, beauty and durability of workmanship. A specialty is made of the construction of Steam Launches and Yachts, among the most famous constructed by this house being the "Sakonnet," "G. G. Green," the "Dream" and the "Wawayanda." A building of two floors (80x60 feet in dimensions) is occupied, an employee force averaging about 6 to 7 kept busy, and every facility possessed for the execution of the finest work in the lines undertaken by this old and reliable house. Both Mr. R. A. Morgan and his son Mr. J. W. Morgan are natives of Noank, and enjoy the highest esteem of their fellow townsmen.

J. W. Rathbun, Dealer in Flour, Grain, Feed, Coal, Ice, etc., Teaming of all kinds, also Livery Stable Keeper, Noank, Conn.—The business conducted by Mr. J. W. Rathbun is one of the most important and largely patronized in this vicinity. It was established by Mr. J. W. Rathbun in 1873, and has been under his sole management during the last sixteen years, in which he has built up a wide, valuable and growing trade. He does both a wholesale and retail business in Flour, Grain, Feed, and Coal, of which he carries a large and reliable stock. In his Livery business, he has on an average eight horses and eleven carriages and employs three men. This department of his business occupies two barns each with two floors (60x40 feet in dimensions) and three sheds each about 30x25 feet. He also conducts an Ice business in which he employs three extra men and uses three ice houses with a capacity of about 3500 tons. Through these various channels, Mr. Rathbun has built up an extensive and growing trade, and gained a wide reputation as an enterprising and reliable business man. He is a native of Noank, and has held various town offices, among them those of Assessor, Weigher, Pound keeper and Constable, which latter he still fills with ability and the confidence of the citizens.

J. E. Stark, General Blacksmith, Horse-shoeing done in first-class manner at lowest rates, Noank, Conn.—We learn that among the earliest of all human industries was that of the blacksmith, and since the days of antiquity it has held a most honorable and essential place in the industrial economy. Mr. J. E. Stark has carried on this work here with growing reputation and success since 1884. He has just entered into new and enlarged quarters, which when entirely completed will include two large floors 75x35 feet in dimensions, and extending out over the water so as to give better facilities for ship-ironwork. This branch of business has been Mr. Stark's specialty from the first, and he will now have improved advantages for meeting the increased amount of repairing work he is continually receiving from vessels coming in here for repairs. Mr. Stark is an experienced and first-class general blacksmith and horse-shoer, and has built up an unsurpassed reputation in these lines. He intends soon to inaugurate a carriage-making business and has about completed facilities for the building, painting and repairing of carriages and wagons. At the present time he employs one assistant but the extension of business in the immediate future will require several more. Mr. Stark is a native of Annapolis, Nova Scotia, and since his residence here, has won a wide spread and well deserved reputation for business ability and sterling character.

L. L. Park, The People's Market, Dealer in Fresh and Salt Meats, Beef, Pork, Mutton, Lamb, Veal, Hams, Poultry, etc., Noank, Conn.—There is no department of trade in which there is greater need of thorough experience and inviolable fidelity than in that of meats, the health of the consumer, as it were, being placed in the hands of the dealers in this staple, and the conditions of care and precaution to be met are manifold and delicate. That Mr. L. L. Park has ably fulfilled these conditions is evidenced by the confidence of his towns-people. He has conducted his meat business here since 1870, being originally alone, then for a few years a member of the firm of C. H. Rathbun & Co., and since 1886 has had sole charge of the business again. He is a native of Noank and well-known and respected by its people. His trade requires 2 assistants, and in his neat store, whose dimensions are 18x40 feet, can be found a reliable stock of fresh and salt meats, including Beef, Pork, Mutton, Lamb, Veal, Hams, Poultry, etc. Mr. Park has a fine, modernly fitted refrigerator in which his meats are most carefully preserved. Special pains are taken that the stock shall always be in the best condition and those placing their custom at this established and reliable stand may be assured of prompt attention and good satisfaction.

Wm. Palmer, Dealer in Patent Medicines, Fruits, Cigars, Stationery, etc., Main Street, Noank, Conn.—The enterprising business conducted by Mr. Wm. Palmer has been established here since 1885, and during that time has been under his sole management. Since the start certain fundamental principles of business, strict integrity and fair dealings united with care and forsight have commended this establishment to the hearty confidence and support of the citizens. A considerable retail trade has been built up in Cigars, Stationer's Goods, Fruits, Confectionery, and especially Patent Medicines, of which a large and select stock has been constantly maintained. The leading proprietary articles and houses are well represented, and Medicines for all ordinary diseases will be found here. A tasty well arranged store, 25x40 feet in dimensions, is occupied and a nice display of stock made. All those desiring articles in the lines here represented will find it both a pleasure and profit to examine the stock of this reliable establishment, and will meet with good service and accommodation. Mr. Palmer is a native of this place and enjoys the esteem as well as the business respect of a large circle of acquaintances and friends.

NARRAGANSETT HOTELS,

WATCH HILL. R. I. WM. HILL, Proprietor.

Of the many beautiful resorts on the New England coast there are none which have so rapidly advanced in popular favor as the PLIMPTON HOUSE at Watch Hill since it came under the control of the present proprietor some 4 years ago. Entering upon his duties with an experience of 25 years as a landlord of first-class hotels, Mr. Hill has made the PLIMPTON and its annexes a favorite resort for families who come year after year. Starting in 1885 with the PLIMPTON, which was then but one-half its present size, the success of the first year was so great that it was enlarged in 1887 by the addition of 60 fine rooms —a large music hall, with a magnificent floor for dancing, and a kitchen that has no superior at any summer resort on the coast. The capacity of the house, although doubled, was still too small, and the present season, therefore, the NARRAGANSETT — one of the adjoining houses — was leased; these affording accommodations for over 250 guests, besides many from neighboring cottages. The location of the PLIMPTON is unexcelled, the proximity to the beautiful bay renders it not only easy of access to the steamers, but affords unrivalled accommodations for yachtsmen, while the bathing beach and the other hotels are within easy walking distance. The rooms are well furnished, and have gas and ample closet room. The sanitary arrangements of the house are unsurpassed, the drainage having been approved as "first-class in every respect" by the State Board of Health. The fine table is not the least attractive feature of the Plimpton, and is managed with liberality and intelligence. A number of first-class cooks, under a competent *chef*, prepare a very attractive bill of fare, while the service is all that could be desired. The music, which is conceded to be the finest at Watch Hill, affords every opportunity for dancing in the afternoon and evening. Taken altogether, the increasing popularity of the Plimpton and its annexes, is not to be wondered at. The transient rates are from $2.50 to $4.00 per day, but special arrangements will be made for the season or for families.

For terms or information, address
WILLIAM HILL, Proprietor, Watch Hill, R. I.

www.ingramcontent.com/pod-product-compliance
Lightning Source LLC
Chambersburg PA
CBHW021523270326

41930CB00008B/1061

* 9 7 8 3 3 3 7 2 3 6 6 7 0 *